# GANG TO GLAM
## Who the F*ck is Cheree Leon?

**CHEREE LEON**

ISBN NUMBER: 978-1-7398930-8-8


For media enquiries, please contact: fam@glamgirlmedia.com

# DEDICATION

This book is for Leon, Skiba & Mum

# CONTENTS

# INTRODUCTION

When I was eleven, standing on a dirty street corner in Birmingham selling drugs, I could not have imagined my life how it is today. I was brought up to believe you'd made it if you got a council house – that was the loftiest goal any of us street rats had. Perhaps, if I'd not had so much responsibility, I would have eased into that life and wore it like a pair of comfy slippers but I'm not sure they would have fit properly.

I seemed to have a drive inside. A burning that had nothing to do with anger but more to do with who I was born to be. No matter what happened, I kept moving forward, stepping over, climbing up, bursting through and on seeing how determined I was, life gave me a hand, clearing the path for me. Everything I ever dreamed of being, I've been.

To be fair, Author was never on the list, but here I am…

# 1 BETTING ON THE WRONG HORSE

When you were a child, did you ever want something so badly that you convinced yourself you'd get it? I did, and the reason I was so sure was that an adult had told me so. Best of all, my horse was due to arrive on Christmas Day…

My excitement that December morning was uncontrollable. I had been up since it was dark, pestering Mum until she had no choice but to get up and get me a carrot. Then, I ran to the condensation-covered windows of our Birmingham council flat, clutching that carrot, and there I waited, for the first glimpse of my horse.

Jumping from foot to foot, rocking from side to side, I danced without spinning or twirling because I didn't want to take my eyes off the street outside, not for a second. I concentrated hard, straining my ears for any distant clip-clops. And I needed a wee, but I held on to it and waited … and waited … and waited.

A few hours later, the buzz of excitement had faded, but I still hadn't realised it wasn't coming. I kept looking out of the window. I kept straining my ears. I kept hoping Irish Jimmy would turn up any minute, holding the reins. But when bedtime came around, it sank in … adults told lies.

The tears were hot and steamy, making my nose snotty. I sobbed so much my chest hurt. I felt betrayed by both Jimmy and Mum, and something inside me shifted. That day, a little piece of my innocence trotted off like the horse that never was. Five was too young for those kinds of lessons.

The night before, Mum had thrown a house party, and as usual, all her pub friends were there. The loud music woke me, and I got up, wandering through clouds of cigarette smoke in my pink nightie, looking for Mum. She was dancing with Irish Jimmy, her long blonde hair falling around her shoulders, her long legs showcased by a little black skirt, a fag in one hand and a glass in the other. I pushed through people to get to her and tugged at her skirt. She looked down, told me to go and get some lemonade from the kitchen, and carried on dancing. I didn't want lemonade - I wanted the noise to stop before it woke Leon and Paul, my two little brothers. I tugged at her skirt again, but this time, Jimmy decided to get involved. He bent down, grinning drunkenly, and asked, 'What is it you want for Christmas, darling?'

'I really, really, really want a horse,' I told him.

Jimmy kept grinning. 'If you go back to bed, I'll bring you a horse in the morning. I promise.'

My little heart filled with happiness, and I quite forgot about the noise. Going back to bed, I fell asleep with a big smile on my face because I was so happy.

I don't remember what time I got up on Christmas morning - it was still dark. The house was spotless, though, and you'd never have known there'd been a party if not for the smell of spilled lager on the carpet and dirty ashtrays creeping through the lavender-scented Pledge. Mum might have been a party girl, but she always cleaned up before going to bed - always.

I can't remember anything else about that Christmas Day apart from feeling heartbroken - clearly, something about it had dug down deep.

As for parties, there were always plenty at ours. Indoors when it was cold and in the garden when it wasn't. Mum was a massive reggae fan, and her regular haunt was a place called Monte Carlo's. She had met many musicians on their way up in there, like Maxi Priest and the UB40 boys, so the parties generally started as jamming sessions. Back then, council fences were just short sticks and a bit of metal wire, so the neighbours joined in too. As I got older, I often sang along with them. Singing was in our genes as we got it from Nan – she'd been a singer in the war, and I could imagine her lovely voice being a great comfort to the soldiers.

Nan was my favourite person in the whole world. I adored her. She was a strong woman who had raised ten kids and was striking to look at. Tall and curvy, with long white curls falling down her back and whenever I looked at her, I just thought, 'Wow.' She was not your typical Nan and there was no apron or tan tights, but she did have massive boobs and she kindly passed them down to me.

Even her style was different from other nans. She wore long, fitted dresses like a movie star, and when she hugged you, the scent of musk, Imperial Leather, and leftover smoke from her Park Drive cigarettes was intoxicating. I understood why Grandad kept getting her pregnant - he just couldn't help himself.

They lived in a big five-bedroom house in the nice part of town, and their home was stylish, welcoming, and smelled of Old Virginia from Grandad's pipe. Visiting them was such a treat, especially on Sundays when the whole family gathered in their pink living room for dinner. Surrounded by pink flock wallpaper, we'd sit on dusky pink sofas and chat while we waited for food. You could hear pots and pans clanking and Nan singing as she chopped and stirred. Normally, she belted out Patsy Cline's *Crazy* and I always stopped chatting to listen to her rich tones. Grandad's job didn't start until the meat was on the table. That's when he got busy with the carving knife. He was a big, strong man, covered in tattoos of swallows and tigers from the war. Captured and tortured by the Japanese, they had hung him upside down and slashed him with machetes. I think the tiger tattoos represented that experience because when I asked him about the huge slash marks on his arms, he told me he had fought off a lion.

My grandparents had a very traditional relationship - him sitting in his armchair, smoking a pipe, while she waited on him hand and foot. That was normal for their generation, and they seemed happy with their roles and still very much in love.

On warmer days, I would be out in the flower filled front garden. There were so many flowers, it looked like painting, but it seemed to me there were too many going to waste, so I'd pick handfuls, tie them in bunches, and sell bouquets to passers-by for a little sweet money. Once a hustler…

We kids loved being at Nan's, especially since it was never cold and there was always plenty of food, unlike at our house. We were always freezing, and there was never much food. There was always booze in the cupboard but not much else. When things were bad, I would wake my brothers early and tell them to be ready for the milkman. We'd all listen out until we heard the clink of bottles being set on doorsteps, and then Leon and Paul would sneak around, lifting milk and bread. That was survival 101 - it was how we got by, especially on days when there was no money for the electric meter. That happened far too often, and in the depths of winter, we huddled together in bed for warmth.

As the older sister, I felt a huge responsibility to take care of my brothers and I'd figured out a way to do it. With my best grown-up handwriting, I wrote lists for Raj, the owner of our exotic corner shop. Walking in there felt like being transported to India on a whiff of curry and spice. Raj would take the note from me, believing it was from Mum, and he'd start putting things together - usually bacon, eggs, and beans, which was what the boys mostly ate. As I got older, fags were added to the list, but never a full packet, just singles. I'm sure he knew they were for me, but the world didn't care about such things back then.

Our circumstances forced us to grow up quickly, and we became street-savvy early on. Knowing how to survive was essential, and with all the freedom and lack of supervision, it wasn't long before I turned to crime. Not that I thought of it as 'crime.' It was more like joining the family business as Uncles Paul and David were already well known for it. I loved them unconditionally, whether they were on the straight and narrow or more crooked than a witch's nose. They looked out for us, and we needed that.

At the age of eleven, I had my own pitch outside the red telephone box on Witton Lodge Road, selling resin in five- and ten-pound draws or single spliffs. Everyone smoked resin back then, and mine was supplied by Uncle David. My business uniform was a hooded tracksuit and trainers, looking every inch the council estate grafter. The money I earned put food on the table for my brothers and sisters, and I never spent much on myself. But the temptation and opportunity to smoke the gear was there, and honestly, it mellowed me out. At eleven years of age, I was a stressed-out kid, having felt the heavy weight of responsibility on my shoulders for years already.

I think we all look back on years gone by and wonder why we didn't do or say something at the time, and I often wondered why I'd never told my nan. All I can think is that having seen what happened to families' social services got involved with, I was too scared to open my mouth to anyone, just in case.

Before all the things I've told you so far, in the first four years of my life, I had a dad. A handsome, charming, funny, Irish one who had loved my hot fox of a mother. I mean, how could he not have fallen for her natural curves, her glamorous style, and her upbeat, party-girl personality? That was her with him but when it came to us, she was as strict as a Catholic nun, and if you caught her on a bad day, you'd better run. To this day, I'm sure the outline of her slipper is still on my arse.

In those beautiful days, it was just the five of us. My charming Dad, hot-fox Mum, an obsessed-with-dancing me, an excitable and cheeky Leon, and a quiet, calm Paul.

Sadly, it didn't last, and Dad left us. When he did, Mum started to go out all the time, and I had no choice but to step into her shoes. As females, we do that naturally, don't we?  No matter our age. These days, when people say I'm a good mum, I tell them it's because I've been practising since I was five years old.

It could not have been easy being a single parent in those days, but even when she did 'mum-like' things, they left a different kind of mark. Like she'd pick me up from school in tiny skirts, low-cut tops, and sexy high-heeled boots, and everyone would stare at her - it embarrassed me. Those people were probably jealous of her then, and if it happened these days, well, no one would bat an eyelid, would they? The feelings I have about this subject are conflicting. On one hand, I'm a strong woman who doesn't give a crap what people think of me, but on the other, I'm Skylar's mum, and I'd never want her to feel embarrassed about me. Parenting is such a balancing act, and I'm sure we all struggle to get it right. What I know for sure is that back then, people didn't make such a fuss about kids because they just didn't carry as much importance in the world as they do now.

When I was a kid, it was normal for parents leave their kids outside the pub with a packet of crisps and a Coke, leaving them to entertain ourselves. One time, Mum left me for so long that I ended up in hospital with pneumonia, but it wasn't considered neglect or abuse, it was just life at the rough end of the street, and it happened all over the country - but that doesn't make the experience any less traumatic. Things like that hardened the kids and you could never call my generation snowflakes. Still, having been through it myself made me even more protective of my brothers. I never wanted them to feel how I had.

When Dad left us, he didn't just scarper and never look back. He went and got himself a new wife, Jackie, and when he came to take my brothers on days out, he'd bring her. Those were horrible days for me. It felt like torture watching them load into Dad's convertible, all smiles and happiness as if they were staring in car commercial. As they drove off, my little heart would ache and I'd quietly whisper to myself, 'Why doesn't he take me?'

Every time this happened, I got sadder, and it created a dull ache in my chest. This was my earliest experience of heartbreak, and the scars it left behind were painfully triggered many years later when my own daughter's dad left. I understood that pain, and I would have done anything to protect her from it if I could have.

Now the world has progressed, and conversations today are much more open, but when I was little, things weren't discussed with kids. Adults never explained anything to us, so it was quite a surprise to me when I learned the truth … and then I wished I hadn't.

One summer's day, Dad turned up alone and asked for me. My heart started fizzing - finally, it was my turn, and it was just the two of us - no brothers, no wife. Maybe that should have set off alarm bells for Mum because if she'd known why, she would never have let me go. Excitedly, I grabbed Dad's hand tight as we walked out to the car and like a gentleman, he opened the door and closed it behind me. That whiff of Jazz aftershave had sunk its way right down into the seats, and the smell was so comforting to me.

Everything in me was fizzing with excitement at spending the day with him. But that's not how it went down. We'd only driven a little way from the house when he stopped and parked up by a grass verge. *Why had we stopped?* I looked at him, confused, and he said he had something to tell me. I wondered if he was getting me a horse, and the fizzing got fizzier. But then he told me that he was not my dad, and that was why he never took me out with my brothers. He wasn't cruel about it, but he didn't sugar-coat it either.

It took a minute or two for these words to sink in, and when they did, my happy little face fell. My heart got heavy, and I wondered why Mum had never told me. I felt angry that she'd let me believe he was my dad, and I think I felt embarrassed too. All these big thoughts were running through my little kid's brain, and there was a jumble of emotions that I wasn't equipped to deal with at that age. It was overwhelming and making sense of it all wouldn't come until many years later. I sat crying while he turned the car around and took me home. There was a horrible, worthless feeling in my belly and that was the start of abandonment issues that I've carried with me my whole life.

Pain hardens us and makes us strong, and as I got older, that strength became useful. In some respects, it's a blessing because when you go out into the big wide world, there are plenty of sharks are waiting and if you're an innocent lamb, you'll be sacrificed and served up with mint sauce. But not me - by the time I got out there, I was a full-on lioness.

Life wasn't bad. We did have fun times, and the parties at our house never stopped. There were always a lot of adults around and some great characters, like my uncles. Honestly, I could fill several books with their stories, especially about David and Paul. They'd both led dual lives - one on the outside with us and one behind bars. Doing time was normal for them, and they will always be known as the crew who robbed Unigate - that job went down in local history as one of the biggest robberies in Birmingham.

Uncle Paul had a lot of stories about prison, and he liked to tell the one about Ronnie Kray knocking him out when they first met. He served with the Kray twins for a long time, and they became friends eventually. When Nan visited, she'd take extra chocolate for the twins as she worked in the Cadbury factory and could lay her hands on plenty of it. They'd appreciated it so much that one Christmas, they made her an ornament out of lollipops sticks.  It couldn't have been easy knocking Paul out as he was a big man, built like a boxer, with a bald head and a Borstal dot on the side of his face. He'd usually show up at ours in a shiny car and dressed in a suit, but one morning I woke up to find him sleeping on our sofa in his tracksuit bottoms. Later that afternoon, he stood in the kitchen making a stew - his big, tattooed arms on display as he stirred the pot. Mum was listening to her reggae records in the living room, my brothers were upstairs playing, and I was practicing my dancing when there was a loud banging on the front door and a voice shouted, "Police – open the door."

When Mum opened it, five officers in uniform pushed their way in, saying they were looking for Paul who'd escaped from prison. They found him in the kitchen, still standing there, stirring the pot. He didn't even look up.

"Paul Sprason, we're taking you back to prison," one of them announced.

But they let him take a few mouthfuls of stew before they cuffed him, and I could tell there was something about his presence that made them do that. It was weird, exciting, and funny all at once. In my head, I connected some dots and worked out that being a criminal was a bit like being a celebrity. You were treated differently to other people, and I liked the sound of that.

In general, my uncles were good role models, and I learned something from all of them. You might wonder what good things I could learn from the criminal side, but that's easy to explain. What they had were strong family values and loyalty which are simple, yet important characteristics that hold high value.

I had non-criminal uncles too, like Uncle Barry. I'd lived with him and his wife, June, in their lovely house when I was a baby. He'd had a decorating business in Tamworth and did very well for himself. Obviously, I don't remember much, as I was just a baby, but I always feel happy when I smell Johnson's baby powder and I think that's because of them.

After giving birth, Mum didn't do too well, and she'd run off to Torquay. They called it the 'baby blues' back then, but we call it postpartum depression now. Uncle Barry and Auntie Mandy both wanted to look after me, but Barry won. If Many had, my life would have been so different as she went on to have three boys of her own and two of them became performances coaches in the football industry, working with people like Ronaldo. Don't worry though, I did not miss the footballers altogether, as you'll see later...

Before she'd run off, Mum had left me in my pram outside Mothercare and turned up at Nans without me. I think Nan was concerned that it wasn't an accident, especially as Mum had been talking about putting me up for adoption. That's when my uncle stepped in. From what I've heard, my aunt and uncle doted on me, and they would have adopted me, but when Mum came for a visit after six months away, she changed her mind. They said I was covered in baby powder and laying butt naked on a sheepskin rug in their living room. Mum took one look at me and said I was the most beautiful thing she'd ever seen.

She took me back but, if she hadn't, I might never have become an eleven-year-old drug dealer.

But I wasn't the only one getting into a bit of trouble. One night, as I stood on my pitch, I heard the roar of an engine as Leon skidded up beside me in a silver car. He was laughing his head off. At nine, he was too small to see over the steering wheel, so he'd ripped the headrest off and was sitting on it. It was funny, but I panicked and jumped in the car with him, thinking we could go and dump it somewhere. As we pulled away, we saw Mum and I screamed at Leon to turn around, but it was too late; she'd seen us. I opened the door to get out and she was on me, grabbing my hair and yanking me around the other side, so she could get her hands on Leon. Grabbing him roughly by the arm, she then dragged both of us down the street with her high heels clicking and clacking as she shouted angrily at both of us. We knew we were in big trouble, but here's the thing about Mum, she could never ground us because that would mean she had to stay in herself. So, we always got the hard slipper and a lot of threats.

Soon, both Paul and Leon were in the family business, and they'd planned the robbery of a storage shed at the back of a local pub. In the early hours of a Sunday morning, dressed in black like skinny little ninjas, they wriggled through a small window and stole all the booze they could get their hands on. They'd stolen a quad bike the day before and tied a supermarket trolley to the back of it, for piling all the booze in – clever little ninjas. As the sun came up on our Birmingham council estate, the sight of two little boys on a trolley quad, waving bottles in the air and shouting 'get your cheap booze,' put a smile on many faces. And, despite being woken up early, the neighbours loved it. The leftover bottles I stashed around the house, but I don't know why I tried to hide it, mum could smell free booze ten blocks away. Still, I put it in toy boxes and at the back of wardrobes and of course, we drank some. When Mum found out, she went ballistic at us, but she kept the booze and when the police came knocking, she said all her kids had been at home, sleeping. We lived in a 'fell off the back of a lorry,' neighbourhood and no one ever got grassed up.

I know it sounds bad, but for us, making money for food and electricity meant committing crime. We were hungry kids, and Mum didn't really provide. Worse still, she'd started to disappear for for days on end, so what else were we supposed to do? The disappearing made me so anxious, and I kept fretting that one day I'd find out she was dead. But she always eventually came home, reeking of stale cider and too much Taboo perfume and when she did, I'd tuck her up, kiss her on the forehead and make sure there was water by her bed.

Life was looking grim. Mum was an alcoholic, I was a drug dealer, and my brothers were already on the road to prison. The money I made from drugs bought us food, and I had a lot of customers who were friends from the schools I'd been to. Sometimes, when I was on my pitch, my best mate Rhonda would come hang with me, and we'd smoke spliffs and plan world domination. She was a big, tall, mixed-race girl with boobs that could crush you if you hugged her. Rhonda had great thieving skills and she could easily nick ten pairs of jeans in one go. Whenever we planned 'shopping' days, I got the job of 'distractor,' but the one time I became the 'holder,' it went horribly wrong for me.

We'd been on our way to the shops, and I had my baby brother Keith in the pram with us. As we were walking along, we saw a girl on the other side of the road, wearing gold chains. Where we lived, everyone knew not to go out like that - it was just asking for trouble. Rhonda's eyes lit up, and she flew across the road, grabbed the girl by her arm, and told her to take the chains off. There was a tiny struggle, but I think the girl knew it was pointless and Rhonda came back glinting and grinning. All I had done was watch, but then, I put the chains in the pram for safekeeping. We didn't bother going on the rob after that; we went home, and I hid the gold in the wardrobe until we could sort out buyers.

That girl reported it us to the police and she gave such a detailed description of me, they soon came knocking at our door. It was Easter Sunday, so plenty of space for some good old Catholic guilt. That incident got me community service, and I think it woke Mum up a bit. Even though the drink had its claws into her and was slowly stealing her away, somewhere deep inside, she had the foundation blocks of a loving family and I think they jumped up and bit her, reminding her how life should be for a young girl.

My school life was a mess. I'd been to five different schools in one year because I'd developed a behavioural problem. Basically, if someone was rude to me, I'd punch them. That was never my character in the beginning because I'd been bullied when I was younger, but one day, Mum and I were on the bus, and I made the mistake of telling her I was scared of someone. She never said a single word, instead she punched me in the face in front of everyone. The message was clear: fear was not an option. OK, got it.

The catchment area for my school was full of African & Jamaican families, and their girls were often tall and big and built. I was tiny and undernourished looking, so they looked like giants next to me. A lot of those girls were in a notorious gang called the "Inch High Crew," and one day, one of them came for me in class. She'd walked straight over and got so close to me I could smell her breath as she leaned down to cuss me out. From the other side of the classroom the rest of the gang were watching. It was pure intimidation, and I was supposed to slink off so that they could laugh at me. But I stood my ground and one of the gang shouted something about not letting a "honky" get away with that. The girl raised her fist to thump me but in a flash of anger I reacted by stabbing her in the boobs with the Biro I'd been holding.

She was screaming in pain when the teacher came in and sent her to the nurse, and I was told the school would have a word my mum. I knew my mum would be glad that I hadn't been scared. After school that day, as I walked to the bus stop, I heard someone shout "honky," and I realised they were behind me. Running like the wind, I didn't look back and was so lucky to see a bus just pulling away. There were no automatic doors in those days, so I just jumped on it, and as it sped off, I turned around with a cheeky grin on my face and gave them the finger. Did I go back to that school? No, but many years later, I learned more about that gang and realised just how lucky I'd been that day.

Through everything, I kept one happiness. One thing that nothing bad could touch. One thing that was just for me. One thing that took me out of my world and transported me to a place of freedom. That was dancing.

'The Hitman and Her' or 'Top of the Pops' were my inspirations, and I danced to it all in the living room, feeling the freedom of movement and self-expression. I wanted that freedom more than anything - even more than I'd wanted the horse.

The entertainment industry was where I belonged. I could feel it, and dancing professionally was where I'd start. How I was going to make that happen was the problem. There was no money for training, lessons, or schools, and I was still doing community service … my dreams weren't going too well.

Then, one morning, Mum was hunting through pockets and bags for cigarette money when she'd found a knife in my schoolbag. I'd started carrying it around for protection, because 'gang life' was just 'life' where we lived, and getting stabbed or dying was a real possibility. Mum wasn't stupid; she knew the risks herself, but when she was drinking, she didn't worry about anything except where the next drink was coming from. Finding that knife was another sign, and it became the reason why she did what she did.

Before that though, a miracle happened. She met a lovely man who was a good influence on her, and she started to settle down a bit. She'd had boyfriends before, but they didn't last long, and I'd often seen the bruises on her face or grip marks on her arm that they'd left behind. But Andy was a normal bloke with a normal job, and he came home every night and wanted to eat dinner with all of us, like a proper family. It was not long after they met that Mum got pregnant, and they started to build a better life together.

My little sister Toni burst into the world the following Christmas, and that day is stamped in my memory like a bad horror movie. I don't know why I'd been in the room during the birth as it was all blood and screeching. Then there'd been a moment of silence between Mum's cries, and someone screamed downstairs. I ran down to find out what had happened and saw Auntie Linda swaying in the kitchen doorway. Her face was as black as ash, and her blonde hair was sticking up like she'd put her finger in the plug socket. I didn't mean to laugh, but...

Linda was a good auntie, but she had her own troubles. Her teenage daughter Thresa had been born with spina bifida and had to be pushed around in a big blue pram but her other daughter, Tracey was a golden child who got everything she wanted. Life could be a balancing act for Linda, but Mum needed her help that day and here she was ... almost killing herself.  Our oven was a very old model with a pilot light at the back, and it had to be lit with a long match. Well, Linda had turned the gas on first, then hunted for matches and when she'd found a short one, she leaned in, and 'boom'. Luckily, there was no lasting damage, but I'll never forget her face, and in my mind, it did replace the bloodbath memory of childbirth.

Community service continued, and one day, I turned up to find a girl from the Inch High Crew there too. As the only white girl and with my long blonde hair, she'd recognised me from the incident at school and told me they were going to get me bad. But, as luck would have it, Mum had arranged to pick me up that day. You know, I'm not sure I would have survived my early life if there wasn't someone up there watching over me – there must have been. And, even though Mum had been absent a lot from our guidance, in those times when I needed her most, she showed up for me like magic.

I never went back to community service, and Mum changed my name after that. It was great at the time but later, in life, that came back to haunt me.

At the grand old age of twelve, the Inch High Crew had it in for me. I'd been done for holding stolen goods, and I'm not going to sugar-coat it, I was a drug dealer. If I'd looked in a crystal ball back then, I might have seen myself behind bars and that could easily have happened, if Mum hadn't done what she did next.

And that's how I ended up in a van, headed to a sleepy village in the sticks, with Ronnie & Reggie.

# 2 THE BIRMINGHAM SIX

A few days after my lucky escape at community service, I'd got home from school to find the whole house packed up and Mum said we were moving to Devon. She knew if she had given me any kind of warning, I would have had time to plot a way to stay. Clever Mum.

But I didn't mind the thought of Devon at all. We'd been on holiday there, and it was beautiful, but saying goodbye was hard. There were so many tears I'm surprised I didn't drown in them.

In typical Mum style, she'd thrown a leaving party, and everyone came - all the uncles, aunts, cousins, musicians, friends, and Rachel, who I'd met at one of my schools. She'd been a good part of my life, not the druggy crime part. Rachel lived in Brooksville Village with her mum, who was a very glamorous stripper. Whenever I was at their house, I thought her mum was rich because there'd be cash stacked in little piles around the house. I'd been on holiday with them once, all the way to Tenerife, and her mum had paid for me. On our first night, we'd gone out to dinner, and I'd ordered steak and chips. To me then, steak was food for rich people, so I felt very grown-up and excited ordering it. The waiter put my plate down, and I grabbed the vinegar and poured it all over my chips. Then I took a mouthful, and it was disgusting. Having never been abroad, I'd had no idea there was olive oil *and* vinegar on the table. They were both in the same glass bottles and both the same colour. Styling it out, I carried on eating it and didn't say anything as I was embarrassed. It's another reason I should be on the stage because it was vile, yet nobody knew.

I knew I'd miss Rachel, and I was so sad when I heard her mum had died quite young - she'd been a glam inspiration to me. But don't worry, Rachel still has a part to play in my story yet...

When the leaving party was done, and everything was packed, our family of eight squashed into the front of the van and got on the road. The journey was long, and when we weren't fidgeting and trying to get comfortable, we'd played games like 'I Spy'. Paul had been holding on tight to his pet fish all the way, but when we stopped for petrol and us kids started moving around a bit, he'd dropped the bag. We all watched in silence as Ronnie and Reggie fought for breath on the floor. But I wanted to save them, so I grabbed a fork from the dashboard to scoop them up with and accidentally stabbed a fish. I think it was Ronnie, and it was only right that he went first.

Paul went mad and started shouting that I'd killed his fish - we started fighting. By the time Andy got back in the wagon, we were all laughing hysterically but that didn't last, because with a speed limit of sixty mph, the journey took us nine hours!

When we finally rolled into Devon, we saw our house sitting on a hill in Bideford, a tiny village that looked like Emmerdale Farm. It had one pub, one shop, two buses a day, and nineteen other houses. City life was all I'd known, and at first, the lack of anything at all was horrifying. In my head, I started to plan my escape.

The next day, I found a telephone box, phoned my mates (the dodgy ones), and asked them to come and get me. And if that didn't happen, I'd have to go to Plan B and that meant making it all work for me somehow.

On the first day of school, me, Leon, and Paul had been sitting on the school bus minding our own business when the girl behind me stuck chewing gum in my hair. I felt her do it, so I turned around, and she was laughing with her mates. That didn't last long, though, because I punched her in the face. Some of the boys had been laughing too, so Leon and Paul started fighting with them and when the bus driver tried to break it up, Leon punched him in the face. First day of school, and not only had we been chucked off the bus, but we'd also been banned from getting on it again. Luckily, we hadn't been far from school when it was all kicking off, but at the end of the day, we found out it was a two-and-a-half-mile walk. From then on, we had to walk five miles a day. As a city family used to a tough life, dropping us in the back of beyond was bound to cause some disruption, but we'd only been there five minutes when they started calling us "The Birmingham Six."

Country life was slow. There were no stolen cars ragging through the streets and all we saw was tractors and the odd cow strolling lazily along.

Looking back, I realise it was the best thing Mum could have done for me as she'd got me away from a life of crime. That whole experience also changed me as a person, and life changed, this time for the better. It took a little time to tame me, and I think I channelled the cockiness into extra confidence, and that was much more useful.

School turned out okay. I made nice friends, and I also became the 'popular' girl. The other kids had been glad when I'd punched that bus girl because she was the school bully. They'd also loved my Birmingham stories, and they liked my accent, and these things all added to my popularity. And of course, I was infamous as a member of The Birmingham Six.

Even the headmistress had taken a shine to me and that was a complete life turnaround.

By the time I'd reached fourteen, life was much more settled. Dancing was still my passion, and at school, I was excelling at drama. With dyslexia, my maths and English were lacking, but I'd landed the lead role in the school play which was a big dramatic production about a time-travelling woman named Dossy and it took place in wartime. I was so excited about it. On opening night, when I first stepped on stage, my whole family was in the front row noisily eating crisps. That was embarrassing, but it didn't put me off performing, because when I was on stage, I felt like I belonged there.

Because the play was such a success, our drama teacher took it out to the theatre and Dossy ran at the Theatre Royal in Plymouth. We performed it as an afternoon matinee for a few weeks, and it was a fantastic experience for me. I totally loved it.

The experience was empowering. I started to dream of moving to London and going to drama school, but I didn't want to leave my family. There was also the responsibility I still felt for my brothers, as I'd been looking out for them for a long time, Leon especially. He'd gone from robbing cars to robbing tractors, and I know he found it difficult adapting to country life. He'd not made any good friends either … Leon was a proper Reggie (fish out of water). I think the reason it all worked for me is that I was adaptable. You don't go from drug dealer to headmistress's pet without being adaptable, and that's what my childhood had taught me. Once we'd got to Devon, I'd reinvented myself and dropped the bad girl image because I just didn't need it anymore.

Whenever I mentioned London to Mum, she'd tell me there was no money in acting and if I went, there'd be no-one to help with the kids. But she also said while I had great potential to be an actress, she wanted to keep me safe. I know she didn't try to hold me back - she was just telling it as she saw it and I got that.

Since she'd met Andy, the constant going out had stopped, so I had a lot more time to myself. Mum got happy, and we felt like we'd got her back. The move had been good for all of us.

My best friend at the time was Kate, and I met her when she'd been chosen to show me around school on the first day. Kate was very tall, very pretty, and quite adult for her age, and with her long curly hair and braces, she was cute. Her dad was the manager of a Mercedes garage in Plymouth, and the family lived in a beautiful six-bed house in Budleigh Salterton. As her best friend, I stayed there a lot, and I know I corrupted her a little. Whenever her parents were away, I'd convince her to have parties, and I remember one time a boy peed in her big shoe and threw it down the stairs. That was the first time I ever saw her mad, and she picked up that shoe and started beating him over the head with it. It was like a scene from Tom & Jerry, and we all fell about laughing.

Moving into my teens meant boyfriends, and my first was Paul Heyman - good-looking, fast car, older than me. His family were loaded, and they had the biggest house in the area with a swimming pool in the garden. This didn't last long as I was more attracted to bad boys, and Paul just wasn't one. Then came Chris Medlock, who was. His family had moved him down from London because he'd been getting into trouble with the police. That was more like it. He was a cockney-voiced drug dealer, and I was a moth to a flame.

Chris also knew how to throw a party, and he'd do it every time his family were away. It was at one of those parties I met his DJ friend

'Apache,' who became a very good friend of mine. As a boyfriend, Chris was generous, always buying me things like expensive trainers, and he was also smart enough to turn up at our house with lots of booze. This made sure Mum liked him. Clever Chris. Most of our relationship revolved around drinking lots of alcohol and smoking lots of weed.

At fifteen, life was good, but money was scarce. That had to change. Through partying, I'd been making good connections in the music industry, and as I loved clubbing and dancing, I thought I could do something that would combine it all. Back in Birmingham, I'd gone to those under eighteen's raves at the leisure centre with my mates Abby Maltby and Lisa Reynolds. Those nights were amazing, and I'd get totally wrapped up in the music, never leaving the dance floor unless it was to sell drugs. There were some lively hotspots in sleepy Devon, and I could still have fun, but I remembered how great those rave nights had been, and I thought to myself, *I could do that.*

And that's how I ended up putting on an illegal rave in a magistrate's court...

# 3 YES I CAN CAN

Kids like me often become entrepreneurs because, from a young age, we've honed our problem-solving skills. Our problem had been the lack of money for food, so I'd always found ways to make some. Now, it was about supply and demand. I loved to dance, and the kids around me tried to copy my moves. They wanted to learn. So, I set up a little dance school at the local hall. It became popular, and that's when I had the bigger idea: I was going to put on a rave.

For that, I needed some adult help, so I roped Mum in. By now, you'll have realised that she wasn't like most mums. My mum, Marie Palla, believed in keeping things clean and being well put together, and the biggest ambition she had for her children was that they'd get a council house. To her, that was the ultimate security.

But she wasn't stupid, and if I'd figured out a way to make money, she was more than happy to help me. What we didn't realise then was the hall we'd hired was the magistrates' court. In a sleepy town like ours, things were done a little differently, and council buildings often had a dual purpose to serve the community.

We plastered flyers around town and in surrounding villages and on the night of the rave, around three hundred kids showed up. DJ Apache set his decks up on the magistrates' bench, and Mum bought cans in bulk, which she sold to the kids. Ivybridge was proper raving that night – it was mental. And, I'd made good money and had a blast. So, I set the date for the next one.

I'd expected the second rave to be even better than the first, but it didn't go to plan. There were around four hundred kids this time and a lot of them spilled out onto the street. Things were getting out of control, and someone called the police. When they'd arrived, there were drunk and stoned underaged kids dancing and whistling in the street and some were chucking up on street corners. We were lucky Mum was there as she told the police it was a kids' party that had gotten out of control. Thankfully, we got away with it, but it killed the venue.

We didn't give up though. Why would we when we had the moors on our doorstep? All that open space, with no one around for miles sounded perfect. Apache took his DJ equipment and a generator, and as word got around, we had crowds of us dancing happily until the sun came up. It was magical – though some of that magic came from the mushrooms we'd picked. We'd gather clumps of them, take them to Chris's place to brew and bottle, and store them for rave night. Weed was better, but whenever I'd taken mushrooms, things would get a bit weird, and I didn't like the out-of-body experience. One night, I had a bad trip and was convinced I had chickenpox. Another time, I thought I was falling off a cliff and someone found me lying on the grass, digging my fingernails into the dirt, trying to hold on. It was horrific and my long nails were filthy and caked in dirt. It scared me so badly that I never touched them again.

We didn't charge for raving on the moors – it was all for the love of music and we danced our hearts out in the massive open space under the sky. And the beauty of it was, anyone could turn up and join in. It was magic.

I was still with Chris then, but one night, his friend Simon came, who was an amazing dancer - I was instantly drawn to him because of that and the attraction was immediate. We danced together all night, and the next morning, when Chris crashed back at his place, I stayed up talking to Simon. Suddenly, he kissed me, and the problem was, I liked it.

Even though Chris and I made a great couple, like a proper Bonnie and Clyde, I knew that if I fancied Simon, I shouldn't be with Chris. On the day I broke up with him, he'd gotten a tattoo on his arm that read 'Cheree' - I felt awful but I knew it was the right thing to do, even when he cried.

As I got older, I became more ambitious, and boys weren't my focus anymore. To make my ideas work, I needed to make money, and that's how I ended up cleaning caravans on Burgh Island.

Have you ever been to Burgh Island? If not, I'd recommend it – it's one of the most beautiful places you can imagine. For me, it holds special memories because that's where we'd go for our family days out. Mum would make packed lunches, and we'd all pile into the van, never knowing if there was enough petrol to get us back home. Those days out were often lived on a wing and a prayer. But if the van did start spluttering on the way home, you could guarantee there'd be a tractor somewhere and dad could siphon petrol from. It was one of the perks of living in the sticks.

Around that time, my best friend was Fat Michelle (that's what she called herself). She was a couple of years older than me, and she had a car, which made life a lot easier when it came to travelling to and from the site. Before we start cleaning, we'd drink a little Lambrini, which seemed very sophisticated back then. Then we'd crank up the volume and clean, dance, and laugh the time away. The caravans didn't have carpets, so I'd simply spray the floors, throw down a towel, and dance on it to clean. We made work fun. On payday, we'd go clubbing, but I always contributed to the 'family day out' fund, and then we'd celebrate by putting petrol in the van. I have such wonderful memories of that time when we were all together and happy.

Some days, when my family were on the beach, we'd take a break and join them. The boys loved swimming, and I loved watching them and I often thought about them rolling into our estate in Birmingham with all that stolen booze. While it was funny, I much preferred seeing them free and having fun in the sea. On those days Mum would sit on the beach drinking cider and Michelle, and I lounged around sunbathing and planning our nights out.

One such day, a weird mist rolled in, and we couldn't see the boys through it. The warning siren started wailing, and we began to panic. This part of the sea was known for having two currents that could be dangerous, and there were warning signs everywhere. As the mist got thicker, Mum started screaming, and I felt sick. My heart pounded in my chest like it might burst. Luckily, the lifeguards were very experienced and had been in the water the moment the mist rolled in. They rescued my brothers, and we saw them being carried through the vapour like a scene from a movie. It was dramatic and scary, but a big relief to see Paul and Leon safe. Now, as a mum myself, I know how it feels when one of your kids is in danger, and it's the exact same feeling I had that day. I think there will always be a part of me that is mum to Leon and Paul.

When I wasn't cleaning caravans, I worked in a fruit and veg shop after school, and I'd also started waitressing on weekends. The venue was a western bar built in a barn in the middle of nowhere. On the first night, I was amazed at how many people turned up, completely dressed for it. It was a big deal for them, and they certainly knew how to enjoy themselves. That got my brain ticking so I pitched an idea to the owner who loved it. Next, I recruited my mates, and we learned the 'can-can', then we started putting together a show. Over time, we added bits here and there, and eventually, we even had a choreographed bar fight. It was so much fun, even though it was me getting hit over the head with a bottle.

On Saturday afternoons, we had the place to ourselves for practice. Being alone in the venue gave us access to an open bar and, after a few drinks with the girls, our shows became a bit more fun. We were never falling-over drunk though. They say, 'Do what you love, and you'll never work a day in your life.' Well, that was true for me when I was dancing or performing, and I knew that's what I wanted to do with my life.

Things started to take off in that direction when Mum replied to an advert for glamour models in the Yellow Free Ads.

And that's how I ended up dining on the HMS Brave with the Captain and five hundred seamen.

# 4 BROKE BRAVE & BOOB BENEFITS

Mum had sent photos of me posing in a little outfit from Topshop and she'd also added a couple of years to my age - overnight, I became seventeen.

The agency came back with a 'yes,' and they booked me for a job with Navy News – which, as it turned out, required a swimsuit!

The bright yellow one mum had for me was truly horrible, but it was all I had. She'd put a yellow flower in my hair and a pair of her high heels on my feet. They were two sizes too big, and the heels were scrapped at the back, which made me embarrassed. Not used to high heels, my knees kept knocking together as I practiced walking in them. Mum was holding me up, and I was so nervous and cold. We were on a ship at sea, and the breeze was freezing, leaving me covered in goosebumps. Ever practical, Mum just draped her black mac over my shoulders, and that's how I walked out to greet five hundred sailors.

There I was, fifteen years old, in ugly swimsuit, worn-out heels, and goosebumps all over me, wobbling along the ship's catwalk with Mum's black mac blowing out behind me like a superhero cape.

The two other models were older than me, and they were so kind, making sure I knew what to do and helping me feel calmer. Once we were in position, smiling and waving, the men cheered. It was then that I realised I was still wearing the mac and had been clutching it over my chest. As I shrugged it off, five hundred men started whooping and whistling like crazy and that was when I realised the benefits of boobs! It was such a rush - a natural high that had nothing to do with drugs but got me addicted anyway. *I belong up here*, I thought.

When the Captain joined us, we had a photo shoot and then wrapped up and soon I was getting changed into my dinner dress. I'd never have been able to afford a proper one, but as always, Mum bought one from a charity shop and spent the night altering it, making it beautiful. That first booking felt like a rite of passage for me - the girl in the tracksuit had burst out of her cocoon and unfolded her wings. There was no going back.

We'd been invited to dinner on the ship and walking into the dining room that night felt like stepping into a fairy tale. Crisp white linen covered the tables, crystal glasses were set at each place, and polished silver cutlery gleamed in the candlelight. Every single head turned as we walked in – all five hundred of them. It was unreal. Like, pinch-me unreal.

The captain was waiting for us, and we were seated at his captain's table, as black-suited waiters in bow ties poured our wine. The three-course menu was a first for me. Prawns were served as a starter, but I didn't like them, so I just picked at the salad and bread roll. Then steak for the main course, with thick-cut chips. Throughout the meal, the waiters kept topping up our glasses, making sure they were never empty. Mum loved that. After a delicious chocolate sponge dessert, we were finished, and Mum needed to be 'helped' off the ship. Having fully taken advantage of the never-empty wine glass, she was completely wrecked. The steward helped her as I pulled her into the cab that had been booked for the job. It must have cost at least fifty pounds, and it was all paid for. That really impressed me at the time, and in my tipsy state, I said to myself, *this is the life.*

It had been a wonderful experience and gave me a glimpse into the kind of life I wanted. From a young age, I'd visualised a life far different from the one I'd been born into, especially when things were bad at home. When Mum had been drinking too much or fighting with some man, I'd listen to the thumps and shouting and tell myself that when I grew up, I was going to be somebody - I was going to have an amazing life. That night on the ship gave me a clearer picture of what it could look like.

The job had been fantastic for me, and because it had been in the papers, people started recognising me when I went out in Plymouth. It gave me a tiny taste of celebrity life, and I loved the flavour.

Modelling had been added to my skillset, but I still wanted to be a dancer, so I auditioned for an agency called 'Eye Catchers,' which represented both. They asked me to wear a leotard for the audition, and once again, Mum found me one in a charity shop. The only problem was that it had a thong back, which felt very intrusive.

When I got on stage, I was nervous as hell, but as soon as the music started, I let go and did what I did best - danced my heart out to the sound of 'No Limits.' Since I still hadn't mastered dancing in heels and didn't have any at that stage, I wore trainers and gave it everything I had. But then, they asked me to do it again in shoes. I wore Mum's and while it wasn't perfect, I styled it out.

The owner of the agency, a friendly woman in her fifties with thick-rimmed glasses, told me I'd done well, and she signed me. She also said I needed to practice, practice, practice dancing in shoes and to get some that fit. That's how my dancing career began, and with all the confidence I had then, no one questioned my age on jobs. I also had 'that' look – long blonde hair, big blue eyes, big boobs – I'd say it was the look of the era, but I've learned that it never really goes out of fashion.

At my very first dancing job, I was sent to a PA at Ritzys, and it was there Lovestation saw me.

And that's how I ended up acting in the music video for 'Best of My Love.'

# 5 THE BEST OF MY LOVE

Auditions were coming in fast, but without any transport, it was difficult, so I roped Michelle into driving me around. I paid her, of course. Most of the jobs were in Plymouth, which was about a twenty-five-minute drive.

As we grew up, we started hitting the big raves. DJ Apache was making a name for himself, and he was no longer just a bedroom DJ.  We dated for a while and wherever he gigged, I danced. One night, he was on the same line-up as DJ Hype, a legend on the rave scene and huge in Plymouth. Hype was headlining that night, and I was mesmerized by him. It wasn't just his music that got me, it was his cockney accent and that made me think, *Goodbye Apache, hello Hype.*

The Lovestation gig came up, and I brought my dance crew into it. We were all set to meet in London the night before the shoot. However, I decided to go with Hype to a big gig in Milton Keynes first, thinking I'd make it to London afterward.

I managed to get to Reading Station, and Hype rolled up in his shiny new BMW, with Johnny Jungle and his girlfriend, Kerry. Johnny got in the front, leaving us girls in the back, chatting, and laughing. Kerry was this stunning, tall girl who always looked elegant, no matter what she wore. But that image of her was about to change.

We were chatting, giggling, and smoking weed when she pulled a little bag out from her pocket. Leaning in like she was sharing a secret, she whispered, "I've got some ecstasy," then she popped a pill into her mouth and passed one to me. I remembered the Leah Betts story and fear set in, but I took it anyway and just nibbled a tiny bit.

Twenty minutes later, Kerry collapsed. She slumped in her seat and was drooling - I was terrified she might die. I could feel the effects from the tiny bit of pill I'd had, so they must have been strong. I screamed at the boys for help, and Johnny lost it. We found the nearest hospital and spent the night there while Kerry had her stomach pumped. Hype missed his gig, and the whole thing was a disaster. Feeling guilty, I realised I still had to get to London for the music shoot.

Rocking up to Pineapple Studios the next morning looking rough, smelling like weed wasn't my finest moment. best look. The girls rolled their eyes at me, but somehow, I pulled it together and managed to rehearse for a couple of hours before the shoot. Rehearsal drinks were necessary that day.

In the video, Lovestation posted a newspaper ad: "LOVESTATION LOOKING FOR A SINGER." The set had been designed for an audition scene, and in the video, I ended up fighting with the real singer for the lead position on stage. What could've been a disaster turned into a lot of fun, and we nailed it.

Talking about that story reminded me I'd been in some karaoke videos before that. You know, the ones they used to play in pubs that had lyrics over the visuals? I think the company was called Sunfly. I remember being the woman in a plane for Whitney's "I Will Always Love You" and I did one for WHAM. Can't remember which one but there was a lot of stamping.

With all the raving, I'd been spotted by a promoter, and he'd hired me to dance at some of the bigger events. My first gig had around two thousand people in the audience, and it was an incredible rush. Stepping onto that smoke-filled stage, seeing the crowd, and feeling the bass vibrate through me was unreal. I got hooked.

At that event, I met Lisa and Nikki, and we formed a dance troupe called Ultra High Frequency - soon shortened to UHF. Our lives took off from there. We became hugely popular, initially dancing regularly at Dance Planet. But before long, we were booked for gigs all over England, Scotland, and Wales. We even made it to Southend once, though I don't remember which club we went to. Back then, I never imagined I'd end up living there.

Andy, my stepdad, became our driver, and Leon tagged along because Mum didn't want us going anywhere unchaperoned. I was making great connections and earning good money. Mum made our costumes - sexy white Lycra leggings that showed the G-strings underneath, and she'd embellish them with diamonds. We sparkled, and the men loved it. We were dancing in the spotlight, in music videos, and getting featured in magazines like 'One Nation'. The first time it registered with me how far we'd come, I was swinging in a cage high above a stage full of fire.

It was December 1991, and I'll never forget that Dreamscape event at the Sanctuary Festival in Milton Keynes. The venue held around five thousand people, and it was packed. As I was lifted in the cage, I panicked. I'm scared of heights, and the view was terrifying. When I was up it swayed gently, and I felt like I was about to lose it. My mind raced, and I thought about screaming to the crowd for help. But it was too late. The intro to *Firestarter* kicked in, and Keith Flint ran onto the stage, singing at the top of his lungs, "I'm the trouble starter, punkin instigator." The crowd erupted as the stage burned. It was pure madness - an incredible adrenaline rush that shot though me as I started to dance like crazy. I looked over at Lisa to check I wasn't the only one. She had her mouth open, screaming as she flung her blonde hair around. Looked like we were all crazy with excitement and it felt like I was in the middle of a storm made up of magic and electricity - it was so surreal I wasn't even sure we were on earth!

As UHF, we travelled all over the country, and I became good friends with Iks, the owner of Dance Planet. He was a public schoolboy who'd been sent to the UK for a better education, by his Nigerian family. Then he'd started putting on raves and brought in big names like Carl Cox.  As mates, we were inseparable - he was like Charlie, and we were his angels. He'd even let me drive his car and it was worth about fifty grand but I'm not sure he ever realised I didn't have license.

Drum & Bass was huge, and we were one of the first dance troupes on the scene. The crowd fed our energy- they loved us and, the money was great. As I managed and trained the troupe, I got a cut from every gig and made a solid income. And best of all, it never felt like work. We'd got to travel around, stay in nice hotels, do what we loved on stage and then party afterward with the best names in the business. How lucky was I!

Then we started to get regular gigs and our first was at One Nation, a club owned by Terry Stone. He is the legend who plays Tony Tucker in 'Rise of the Foot Soldier' and a producer for the films. Terry also owned 'One Nation' magazine and we were frequently featured in that. He is a lovely bloke and he really helped boost our reputation - I'll always be grateful to him for that.

By now, we were dancing on the biggest stages with the biggest names, like Massive Attack and at one of these big gigs, I met Lip Master Mark. That all started because he'd been shining a laser pen light on me as I danced, following my moves – it was funny. Mark had an infectious energy, and he was a joker, always pulling faces or beatboxing as he kept everyone in high spirits. With Evenson Allen, they were known as 'The Rat Pack,' and they were the first DJ/MC duo on the rave scene. Seeing them in action was exciting as they really know how to hype up a crowd. His laser pen flirting led to us dating and together we were effortless. He was super organised and took care of everything - booking hotels, taking me to events, and getting us into the best parties. This was a lovely time in my life and I'm so grateful I met him. Mark is a true gent and a super nice guy, and everyone should have someone like him in their life, even if it's just for a little while.

The Rat Pack were huge and because of that, we were treated like royalty wherever we went; attending the best parties and always free drinks. When the road we were on split into two different paths, we ended things on good terms, but it was a beautiful, magical romance, and I'll always look back on it with a big smile.

Having been so focused on my career, I'd not spent much time with Mum, so, I decided to treat her to a weekend away.

And that's how I ended up on the front-page for having sex eight times a night with a British legend.

# 6 THE PRICE OF A KISS & TELL

Mum had always been a huge snooker fan, and back in the day, she was well-known for pool hustling in the local pubs. Her idol was Steve Davis - she was his number one fan. So, I decided to treat her to a girls' weekend in Bristol to see him play.

We had great seats, but as I sat there watching the match, I began to regret my decision. It was incredibly boring, so there was nothing for it but to get up to some mischief. I waited until Steve looked out into the crowd, and when he glanced our way, I winked at him. When he missed the shot, I did wonder if it were my fault. Pleased with myself, I couldn't stop chuckling as I imagined the headline: *"BORED BLONDE BABE BREAKS STEVE DAVIS'S BALLS."*

Tempting fate like that was a bad idea. Steve kept staring directly at us after that. "He keeps looking at us, Cheree," Mum said excitedly. I told her about the wink, and she gasped, "Oh my God. I can't believe you did that." Then, in typical Mum fashion, she said, "Wink at him again, and he might get us some free drinks." So, I did.

That match felt like it went on for days, and I was relieved when it was over but as we entered the foyer, there was Steve Davis, and he was, looking for us. Mum was ecstatic. She shoved a beer mat into his hand and asked him to sign it. I have no idea where she'd found a beer mat or why she had one in her bag, but she always carried the most random things. After signing, Steve handed it back to her and quickly pressed a folded-up piece of paper into my hand, then he rushed off.  I opened the note. It said, "Meet me later. Here's my phone number. Don't tell anyone." Mum was thrilled and she urged me to go. So, I did.

I would never have said Steve Davis was my type. For one he was much older than me but there was something about him and that surprised me. He was charismatic, and we shared common interests, like our taste in music. That first night, we talked for hours, drank, and smoked weed, and I got to know the more interesting side of Steve. He wasn't boring at all.

Funny how paths cross isn't it? Many years later, Steve became a DJ and headlined a gig with Lip Master Mark. They'd started chatting about the old days and I became a hot topic of conversation – It was Mark who told me about it and after what happened, I didn't think I'd want to be a fly on the wall.

After the first night with Steve, I thought that was it, but he kept messaging me, asking to meet up again. At that time, I had no idea he was married - Mum hadn't mentioned it, and it wasn't like today, where

I could learn everything about him on Google. All I knew was that he was a famous snooker player and very wealthy and he seemed to be growing on me. We were seeing a lot of each other but always in hotels and our nights all went the same way. Meet up, smoke weed, and have incredible sex. He thought of me as his little sex kitten, and I felt adored.

You might be reading this and thinking, I was being used. All these years later I'm much wiser and I understand that, but that worthless abandoned feeling I carried with me would stop when I was being adored by someone, even if it was just all about the sex.

It was also fun, and Steve spoiled me rotten, but it all ended very quickly, just before Christmas, and it was all because of his number one fan.

My sister had told me that Mum was struggling for money and couldn't afford presents for the kids. She looked at me with her eyebrows arched, like a Disney villain, and said, "Steve Davis is really rich and famous, Cheree, so if you sold your story, the family wouldn't have a shit Christmas." She was convinced it was a done deal and it was her who reached out to 'The Sun,' and they offered us thirty grand. That was an enormous amount of money, and it was hard to say no to. I pictured my family having the best Christmas ever, and I decided they deserved to be spoiled, at least once in their lives.

The press were desperate for the story. Steve was a massive star, at the height of his career, and they knew a scandal like that would sell papers. They wanted the story before anyone else got a hold of it, so they followed us, ready to pounce. My next date with Steve was already in the diary and I gave the reporters all the details. They plotted up outside the hotel and waited, ready to strike like a disturbed rattlesnake.

By then, my relationship with Steve was in a routine and it always followed the same pattern. We'd meet in a hotel, have an amazing time, then leave separately to avoid being seen together. The last time I saw him was no different. It was fantastic, and when I kissed him goodbye, I made sure it was a kiss he wouldn't forget.

As he left the hotel, the rattlesnake hissed and the paparazzi fired off a series of shots - click, click, click. There was no escaping it, but Steve ran for his life.

The headline screamed: *"SNOOKER WITH A CUTIE AGE 19, EIGHT TIMES A NIGHT WITH STEVE DAVIS."*

The story exploded, hitting every national newspaper. It was so big, it knocked Dodi & Di off the front page and Spitting Image did a skit about it. In today's terms, it went viral.

But that was just the beginning. The Sun put me up in a hotel, did my hair and makeup, and arranged a photoshoot to go with the story. They wanted an exclusive, so they kept me hidden away and I became the highest-paid kiss-and-tell girl of the times. The paparazzi followed my everywhere. They camped outside my brother's school, loitered around the street corners of our village, and even tried to break into our house. I thought, "What have I done?"

Having signed an exclusivity contract meant I couldn't talk to anyone else about the story, or I'd be sued. For thirty grand, I didn't mind. They paid in instalments, with a first payment of five grand. I used it to take the kids shopping, letting them choose whatever they wanted, and it turned into the best Christmas we'd ever had. My brothers and sisters still take about it.

Big things like this come with big consequences, and anxiety started creeping in. No matter where I went, I felt like someone was watching me. If I ran into anyone I knew, the first thing they'd ask was about Steve. If people recognized me on the street, they'd shout things like, "Did you pot his balls, Cheree?"

Then I was at a rave and the promoter recognised me. He pulled me up to dance on stage. I didn't think anything of it as this was normal for me, but then he handed me a snooker cue and the crowd cheered. I felt utterly humiliated.

One of the worst experiences I had was on a TV show called *Late and Loud* with Nicky Campbell. They'd had me picked me up in a limo and made sure there was plenty of alcohol – luring me into a safe sense of security. It was standard practice. Get me drunk, make me feel relaxed, then hit me with embarrassing questions. During the show, Nicky asked me things, but I never got a chance to reply because the man next to me, who was obviously a plant, kept shouting, "You did it for the money, didn't you?" Well, yes, I did! I'd never denied that.

Apart from my family, everyone I met saw me as, 'the woman who slept with Steve Davis.' All the other parts of me seemed to vanish.

At nineteen, we all do things we might regret, and that was one of mine. But if I had the chance to do it all over again, I would. My deep-rooted need to do everything I can for my siblings, no matter the cost, drove my decision. There was nothing personal in what I did. I liked Steve, and he treated me well. Some people might judge me, and some might judge him for pursuing a nineteen-year-old while being married.

But who are we to judge? We all have our reasons for the things we do. After all these years, I like to think that Steve and I could sit down, share a drink, and laugh about it. If you're reading this, Mr. Davis, mine's a bottle of bubbly.

In the aftermath, I went into hiding, but the hate mail and gossip never stopped. There was only one thing left to do - move out of London and back to Torquay.

And that's how I ended up getting my throat cut by 'The Parish Ecstasy Dealer.'

# 7 THE DISTANCE BETWEEN LIFE & DEATH

When I got to Torquay, I felt like I could breathe again. The whole family were living there as Mum had got an exchange. I managed to get a council house and had Paul, Toni & Chloe all come and live with me. Responsibility hung around me like a cardigan that I could never shrug off. But I knew it well and it gave me something else to focus on.

Slowly I started to feel normal again. I opened a baby clothes shop, so I had a business to concentrate on and sometimes, I'd go out dancing. Dancing was my happy place. Then, one night, some bloke danced up to me and shouted, 'you're that snooker girl aintcha.' I shook my head, carried on dancing but turned around feeling anxious. He didn't go away. 'I know it's you. You're the Steve Davis girl.' I tried to ignore him, but he wouldn't leave me alone. Anxiety took over then and I looked around in a panic, then I saw this guy walking towards us. He grabbed the man's arm, pushed him, and told him to leave me alone. It was like a bolt of lightning went off in my head and I realised that was what I'd been missing. Protection. I don't mean like a bodyguard; I mean like a man who knows it's his role to protect his woman. I'd never thought about it that way before. I'd never needed to as my past relationships were all about fun, partying, and dancing. But in that moment, it was enlightening, and a knowing came over me.

I thanked the guy and looked at him properly as I did. Stocky build, shaved head, beautiful white teeth, and a tan. If I had to guess his name, I'd say it was 'gangster,' but he said it was Scouse Stan.

 As I got to know him more, I started to notice how people were reacting to him and it triggered my memory. I thought about the day the police came for Uncle David and had let him eat his stew. I realised Stan had the same kind of presence about him. I could see people were wary of him, and even when he stood with a group of Brummie hard men, they were cautious with their words around him.

It was inevitable that we'd get together and when we did, we started to create beautiful life. Stan loved to travel, and he'd often book holidays and whisk me away. It was when we were in the states that I'd noticed how popular nail shops were which gave me the idea to open one in the UK. A lovely girl named Gemma was working in my clothes shop and she was running it while I was away, so I thought she could carry on when I got back - then I could take the time to train as a nail tech.

Both Stan and I had a lot of club experience, so it was no surprise that we went into business together and started running 'The Eclipse.' We'd been in their one night, chatting to the owner and he'd said the place was on its arse. I didn't hear what he said next as all I could hear then, were the bells of opportunity ringing in my head. *'Let's take it over,'* I said to Stan.

All the connections I'd made over the years paid off. I got great DJs to come down from London. I got my sisters to dance, and we went from two hundred to two thousand people a night in not much time at all. We were rammed constantly, and we started to make a lot of money.

With both had our separate businesses and with the club, we were earning enough money to upgrade our life. First, we found a stunning flat with breath-taking view over the seafront. And finally, after nine attempts, I passed my driving test and Stan had brought me a new Vitara Jeep. If you saw our life back then, you'd have thought we had it all, but sadly, our relationship had started to turn toxic. Stan was at the gym a lot and he was taking steroids, along with recreational drugs. He'd gone from loving everything about me to being paranoid about me. He didn't like what I wore. He didn't like what I said. He didn't like what I did. And if I spoke to a man, even if it was one I'd been friends with for a long time, there would be hell to pay.

One night, I'd invited Nigel Ben to the club to do a set and I'd organised a photoshoot for him and the dancers. I'd been buzzing about, sorting the girls backstage, when Stan came up behind me, gripped my wrist and pulled me off to the side. Then he accused me of fancying Nigel, and I knew this were going to get bad because he was in a roid rage. I could feel the paranoia steaming out of him. I no interest in Nigel whatsoever but there was no convincing Stan and out of nowhere, I heard a loud crack and realised, it was me. Stan had punched me in the face, breaking my nose. Blood was gushing out and I rushed to the toilets to sort it out. He didn't follow me, and he didn't apologise. I mopped myself up and had to go back out there. Everyone looked at me as if to say, *'what the hell happened?'* I just said I'd fallen down the stairs. They all knew I hadn't, but no one was going to challenge the story. And that's the thing with abuse isn't it – people don't know what to say or do, so they do nothing.

Our personal life was not personal anymore and people were noticing the arguments and the bruises. The club's owner asked for a sit down and he told us we were doing an amazing job. But then he said the arguing in public was out of control and it had to stop. This was all happening not long after we'd got into the relationship so, when the owner first told us the club was on its arse, maybe the bells of opportunity I'd heard were really warning bells.

We ran that club for a year while running our own businesses too, and we managed to turn the club around. The Eclipse live on air had been on the Radio 1 Roadshow. We'd smashed out one of the biggest raves on the seafront and we'd grown drum and base and garage nights into a massive success. We seemed to have the Midas touch, but the drinking and partying was destroying us.

It all came to a head one night when we'd got home from yet another party and Stan started getting nasty. I was wearing a white dress that I absolutely loved and knowing what was about to come, I didn't want blood on it if he hit me, so I picked up a knife. 'Don't come near me Stan,' I'd said as I pointed it at him. What happened next was an accident, but it would never have happened if he hadn't tried to hit me.

Raging and shouting, he was getting closer to me. I was still holding the knife toward him, but it didn't stop him – he rushed me, and we struggled, him pushing my arm away. That pushed the knife toward me, and its blade sliced into my throat. Blood gushed out and poured all down that beautiful dress. Slowly I looked up at Stan, horrified. He was as white as a sheet, with his mouth gaping open just staring at me. And then, he ran. Everything happened in slow motion, even my own movements. Thinking if I stayed there, I'd die, I held on to my neck, ran outside and sunk to the floor. I was laying on the grass when the ambulance showed up. It must have been a neighbour who called them.

It's all a little blurry. A bit like waking up from a dream and trying to hold onto a story that constantly shifts. What I do remember is being sewn up and seeing Mum screaming. The doctor said the cut was half an inch from the jugular. Half an inch - that was the distance between my life and death that night. It was far too short for comfort.

Stan must have called my mum and ever since, she'd been going mental. Seeing me with two black eyes, a busted nose and my throat being stitched up pushed her over the edge and she'd called my uncles.

Thinking he'd get done for attempted murder, Stan had gone on the run, but I had no vengeance in me. The knife incident was an accident, and I didn't want to punish him for any of the other things he'd done intentionally. Our toxic relationship was to blame and even thought he'd hit me repeatedly; he would never have cut my throat on purpose – I knew that. The police did arrest him, but I refused to press charges because I wasn't going to let him go to jail for an accident. It was good of them to warn him though - *'Cheree might have dropped the charges,'* they said, *'but be wary of the uncles, cos they'll kill you.'*

The whole thing was a tragedy because we did love each other. We'd created a beautiful life and a successful business but combine our energies and it was carnage. Subconsciously, there'd been a part of me that thought giving a woman a slap every now and then was normal. I'd seen it happen to Mum often enough and I guess that's why I'd put up with it. These days I'm under no such illusion and I've made sure that Skylar has had a completely different life to me – I pray it never happens to her, but I know that if it does, she won't accept it.

We stayed away from each other after that, and I moved back into the house with Chloe and Paul for a while. Then, as crazy as it must have seemed to everyone around us, me & Stan got back together. I can hear you say, 'What the actual fuck, Cheree' but he never lifted a finger against to me again, even though there were a few times when I knew he wanted to. Our relationship lasted for another twelve years, and we grew together through many of life's experiences.

Back together with things going well, we went on holiday to the Algarve, and we were in the bar one night when they had a magician act. Needing a volunteer, he'd picked me out of the audience and ironically, he wanted to cut my head off. It was just a bit of harmless fun, and I still had my head afterwards. I walked off stage and over to Stan and the magician beelined in on him, asking for his watch. It was a Cartier, a real one and I knew Stan did not want to hand it over, but we were standing in a spotlight, and everyone was watching us, so Stan gave it to him. I was so tense at this time because I'd felt the energy change. The magician put his watch in a hanky and smashed the life out of it with a hammer. My shoulders tensed as if I was preparing for an attack. The magician wriggled his hands over the hanky, did a magic spin and pulled out the watch, perfectly intact. Everyone clapped and the magician went back to the stage.

But Stan never clapped, and his face was like thunder, convinced that his real watch has been stolen and he'd been given a fake. I tried to talk sense into him and thought I'd succeeded but back in our room he started kicking off. I could tell he wanted to hit me, and it made me angry, so I picked up a glass and threw it at him. I didn't aim at his neck on purpose, maybe it was karma that did that as that's where it hit. It started to bleed. I'm sure it would have bounced off a normal person's neck, but Stan had a gym neck, and it was rock solid. When he saw the blood, he fell onto the floor and stopped moving, as if he was dead. I had no idea why he did that. I couldn't understand it, but we'd had a lot to drink that night, so maybe that's why.

Soaking cotton wool in TCP, I cleaned him up with it, but he still didn't move or even talk to me. Since the day I'd got my scar, I'd looked at it in the mirror constantly and every single day it upset me. Maybe on a subconsciously level I'd wanted to do the same to him, I don't know. That was the last time I ever lashed out at him.

When he finally got up, we sat for hours and had a long talk about our relationship. We discussed what we thought was wrong with it and why. We talked about what we wanted out of life and the feelings we had for each other. And We talked about how we could make us better. In the end, we agreed that we would never hurt each other again … and we never did.

Me and Stan were back on track and things were good. But good never lasts does it?  Just when we had figured us out, tragedy struck.

Leon had been in prison for nicking cars and when he was released, they moved him into a halfway house. Getting his life back together he'd found himself a beautiful girl called Amy and he'd also got a dog. One day I saw him walking in town and he was wearing a lovely silver jacket that Stan had given him. We had a little chat, but something didn't look right about him, and I asked if he was ok. He told me not to worry but I had the weirdest feeling about it, and I went home and spoke to Stan. I wanted Leon to live with us for a little while. Stan knew my family could be draining and he told me It was time to stop looking after everyone and take more time for myself. But I'd been looking after them my whole life and it was just a part of who I was. He wasn't being unkind, just protective, which was the very first quality I'd noticed about him.

Halfway houses are normally filled with ex-cons or people with mental health problems and in the room next door to Leon, was an ex-heroin addict who had taken a liking to Amy. While I wasn't there when it happened, I can guess how it all went down. The three of them had been drinking and doing drugs and the guy made a cocktail, giving it to Leon. The problem was, it had methadone in it, which is how I know he was an ex-heroin addict. Maybe he gave it to Leon to make him sleepy, so that he could be alone with Amy? That seems likely to me. As Leon had been drinking, and had never taken methadone before, he overdosed and slipped into a coma. My beautiful brother never woke up again.

He was just nineteen years old, and yes, he was a bit naughty, but he was also kind, caring and a beautiful soul. Everyone who knew him loved him and when he died my heart shattered. Leon was never an angel then, but I know he is now.

Because the police hated our family, we were never going to get justice. Leon was well known to them, and they considered him a menace to society. They said it was 'death by misadventure,' and the man who drugged my brother got away with murder.

I'd been at Mums when the police turned up and I saw them walking toward the house. *'Leons dead Mum.'* I'd said - I could feel it. The police told us what had happened and gave us his jewellery. Mum was screaming hysterically, and I was screaming because the pain wouldn't stop. I didn't think about it at the time, but Mum had lost her own brother at the same age, and I can't imagine her pain. When the police left that day, we sat and waited for the rest of the family to come home and one by one, we had to tell them and watch them fall apart. Every single person's pain added to every single person's pain – it was unbearable.

The next day I went to the hospital morgue with my stepdad and Chloe. We all chose to see Leon separately. He lay on a cold steel table, covered in a green sheet that went up to his neck. Only his head was visible but here was no colour in it. I wished more than anything that he would wake up or that I would wake up and find it was all a dream. Putting my hand on his head felt like touching ice-cold stone and I shivered. Then, like I had done all those years ago at bedtime, I bent down and kissed him one last time on the forehead. *'Don't worry Leon, I'll look after everyone.'* I whispered.

Leaving him was hard. It felt like I was abandoning him. I'd helped raise him. I'd changed his nappies and fed him from a baby spoon. I'd cleaned his cuts and kissed his bruises. I'd told him *'No'* when he needed it, even if he didn't listen. I'd put a roof over his head and clothes on his back and he was just as much mine as he was Mums. I'd never felt pain like it before and I don't have the words to describe the depth of it. I just hope you never have to feel it yourself.


Throughout, Stan was a rock. Not just for me, but for the whole family –
he held us all together. He stepped in and stepped up when we needed
him. He even paid for the funeral, which we held in a lovely little
catholic church. Leons send-off was truly beautiful but here was not
enough room inside for everyone who had come to pay their respects
and people were stood in the churchyard. Somehow it made it worse to
see just how well-loved he had been.


After that, I was drunk for six months straight, and I stopped working at
the club. I could not take the pain sober. Somehow, I kept the nail
business going but mostly, I sat around in my pyjama's half of me here
in this world and half of me in some fog. The grieving process was
brutal. Nan came to our place one day and in an accent, I'd always
adored, she was telling me how well I'd done for myself, but nothing
was registering properly. I just nodded, feeling completely numb. As
Nan was Irish catholic, we'd been brought up to believe in God and
going to church on a Sunday, but after Leon died, I completely lost my
faith. Instead, I looked for answers at the bottom of a bottle and did
some crazy things while under the influence, like stripping bare naked
and running out into the streets. I have no idea why I would do that, but
my head had gone.

Stan used distraction to deal with it. He'd book holidays and find ways take me away from it all and he really did everything he could think of to make me happy again – we went back to America, then Tenerife and then we bought a house together – a beautiful three bed house in Torquay. But life had changed forever and there could be no going back to how it was. Grief has no rules. There's no time limit on it and for me, it was a very slow process - I just put one foot Infront of the other and went through the motions. Time moved slowly on and with it our relationship strengthened. We became very much an 'us.'

It was time to move forward with our lives, but we only had six months because Stan went and got himself nicked. He'd gone out one morning and not returned. That evening I got a call - *'Cheree, I'm nicked,'* he said.

He'd been all tied up in drugs and was involved in an operation on The Cook Report. They'd called him 'The Parish Ecstasy Dealer,' and said his MO was stashing the pills in washing tablet boxes! I guess the police had been watching him and putting it all together and so Stan went to prison.

And that's how I ended up running through the streets with a gang of scar faced Zulus.

# 8 FOR YOUR EYES ONLY

When Stan first went to prison, I wondered how I was going to survive financially. Gemma was still running the shop, but it didn't bring in enough to support the life we'd built, or even cover the rent. I decided to give up the flat and I moved into a little two-bed house next to Dodgy Dave. He'd come over from Africa with his wife and three kids, and he was a real character. A wheeler-dealer who sold drugs and did a bit of building too.

At that time, my sister was lap dancing in London, and she suggested I give it a go. I'd done topless modelling and danced for a living, so really, it should have been easy for me. I didn't want to go into London, so I contacted a club called 'For Your Eyes Only,' in Bournemouth. I took my friend Leandra with me to the audition and we both got the job.

Years ago, Mum had nicknamed herself Candy, so I decided that would be my lap-dancer name. That first night I thought I'd breeze through it, but my legs were knocking together with nerves. It didn't last long though and with the music pumping, I got into it - dance after dance after dance. We smashed it and came out with around six hundred quid each. That was how I earned money while Stan was away. After a few months, even my old friend Rachel from Birmingham joined us. Her mum had called me one night, asking if I could sort her out as she'd started taking drugs and getting into trouble. My solution was to get her lap dancing too.

Me, Rachel, and Leandra got into a routine of going to Bournemouth, staying in a hotel for a few nights, and smashing it at the club. I thought all the girls looked so glamorous. They wore long sequined dresses, and their make-up was perfect. I loved being part of it all. We'd be doing our nails, putting on eyelashes, and then everyone would spray themselves with perfume – everyone had it, so the dressing room stunk of Britney Spears.

Visiting Stan in prison was difficult because they kept moving him around, but I went as much as I could. He'd often notice the glitter and I'd have to swerve the conversation as I didn't want him to find out. Because I was lap dancing, I kept a dark tan and used body glitter, but it was a nightmare to wash off. When Stan finally came out, I'd burned all my costumes and had given it up, so there was nothing to find. Buying him all new clothes was funded by my earnings though and as he got settled in, he said he hated the house, and he also took an instant dislike to Dave.

"Cheree, you've moved me from the frying pan to the fire," he'd said. Being that close to a drug dealer was dangerous for him, so we had to move. We got a flat in the Lincolns, which was a lovely, gated complex. I was happy to move for him, but I made him promise not to get into any more trouble.

We settled down again, living a nice life. One weekend, we met a legend from Birmingham whose name was One Eye Barrington. He was a world cage-fighting champion and at first, I hadn't realised he was a proper Zulu Warrior. For anyone who doesn't come from Birmingham, let me explain...

The Zulu Warriors are a gang of football fans who support Birmingham City. They've been around since the eighties and got their name from Manchester City fans who chanted it at them during a match, because most Birmingham City fans were multicultural.

The Zulus were notorious, and like any other organisation, there were different levels, like you'd have in any army - One Eye Barrington was like a general. We were both Brummies, and we got on like a house on fire. He even took me to my first Blues game, and I was the only girl there. After the match, we went to the pub, and the gang all said I was the only girl allowed to go out with the Zulus. That did make me laugh. We'd all grown up on those streets, so it was easy company; we understood each other.

Eventually, Barrington started bringing more Zulus down, and we'd all hang out and talk about the good old days. He became like family - still is. We were talking about school once, and the Inch High Crew story came out. That's when Stan started to understand my past more. I hadn't really spoken about it to him because I'd left it all behind when I created the new Cheree - I didn't want him to know what a rough street kid I'd been. But that conversation uncovered a few layers, and with our newly strengthened bond, I became more open with him.

From the beginning, Stan had got on with firms from all different areas, and his connections were taking us around the world. I'd opened another nail salon called 'CHE Nails & Beauty,' and I trained students in the back rooms.

Around this time, my brother Paul was looking to become a bit of a wheeler-dealer. Maybe he was still dealing with grief, and that was how it was coming out. I'd gone with the alcohol, and it looked like he was going with the crime. I was scared for him, so I asked Stan to put a stop to it.

I tried to steer Paul towards a painting and decorating business, that was my goal. He'd been getting into trouble in town, and there was a gang that had him marked. I knew it was going to get bad, and I couldn't lose another brother. So, I spoke to Barrington, and he arranged to come down.

On the day, we were in a pub on the seafront called Applebee's. It was a trendy bar with four doors leading to different parts of the beach. A group of Scousers started throwing chips at Paul, baiting him into a fight. If he'd have reacted, they would have jumped him en masse, but before it could all kick off, a slow, monotonous sound filled the pub. It got louder and louder, and people started looking around. I knew what it was. I grabbed Paul's arm and started moving towards the door.

The noise grew, surrounding the pub, as if an enemy was closing in.

"Z U L U, Z U L U, Z U L U."

Then, it was as if the lights went out. The whole pub went dark. Marching in through every exit were massive black men covered in scars. I saw Barrington instantly, standing tall and menacing, a line of Zulus falling in behind him. He looked magnificent - like a general leading his army. The pub fell silent. The only sound was the continuous chant of the Zulu Warriors.

People sat frozen with terror. The Scousers who had been taunting Paul were now surrounded, probably wishing they'd brought spare underwear. Barrington looked over at me. I nodded. He motioned towards the door, signalling for me to leave. I grabbed Paul, and we legged it onto the street. That's when I regretted my outfit choice- short skirt and stilettos weren't ideal for running in.

Police sirens screeched, officers jumped out of cars, and chaos erupted. I was trying to squeeze under an Audi TT when a female copper grabbed my hair and yanked me up. Before I could react, a huge black fist swung past my face and connected with her chin. she went down like a ton of bricks. Ding ding.

Paul and I got away. Millions of pounds' worth of damage was done to the seafront that day and it looked like a bomb had gone off. After that, everyone knew not to fuck with us. And I did convince Paul to go straight – he has a thriving decorating business; a wonderful family and he lives happily in Australia.

You might be wondering where Stan was in all this. I'll tell you.

Whenever things were about to kick off, Stan would be nicely tucked away in some old man's bar, drinking, and smoking a cigar. And this time, he was probably buzzed up on cocaine as he'd started taking a lot. I won't pretend innocence because I did it too, just not when things were kicking off. I had to be in the middle of it all. Somehow, I thought being there would keep the people I loved safe.

Stan had a new business now and he was selling Lombok-style furniture. He ran a big manufacturing operation, making copies and selling them at half the price on sites like eBay. The furniture was flying out the door and I was proud of him for getting out of major crime. But I had no idea he wasn't quite all the way out.

Life could get hectic when Barrington was down, but mostly, we lived a calm life, working hard and holidaying in places like St Lucia. For weekends away, we'd started going to Holland as we'd made some great friends there.

And that's how I ended up with a gun to my head, being held hostage by the Russians.

# 8 THE RUSSIANS ARE COMING

Stan was on edge. He was sleeping badly, drinking heavily, and often, when he was at home, he kept getting up from the sofa and peering out the window. There was a lot he kept from me but that was normal. The less I knew, the less I could get in trouble for, if things went tits up. That didn't stop me worrying, and it didn't stop me sensing when something was wrong, like now.

That year, we'd been to Holland a few times and stayed with our friend Jean and his beautiful wife. Jean was an absolute badass. A big man, well-known in his town and whenever we were out and about, people would come over and say hello to him – like paying their respects. I didn't know exactly what he did for a living, but it must have paid well as they lived on a small private housing estate with grand security gates. Their house was a riverside mansion that looked out onto the water.

We'd also met them in Barcelona and had a wild weekend clubbing. It was a big drinking session, but I remember being in this dimly lit bar with Jean's wife. The boys were over at a table with a group of men who looked like gangsters - big men, big muscles, slick dress sense. They said they were 'doing a bit of business.' Us girls were bored and had gone to the bathroom for a cheeky line. I don't think it was cut with much, as it hit me like rocket fuel, and I was instantly buzzing. Back at the bar, I'd found a pole and was dancing around it, like I used to do in Bournemouth. Stan still didn't know about that though. He was looking over at me as if to say, *'What the fuck are you doing, Cheree?'* Well, what I was doing was having a good time dancing. Dancing was just what I did.

A bit later, when we were sitting, I heard Jean say, *"I don't like people who get on it and party too much - everyone needs to be just chilled."* I don't think he was referring to me, but if he had been, he could blame his wife, as it was her who gave me the gear.

Back at the mansion, I'd crashed hard, but Stan and Jean stayed up drinking and talking 'business.' The reason I mention this is because I'm sure it had something to do with what happened later and was also the reason Stan couldn't sleep.

Life was chugging along well in the UK. We lived in a nice house and had money. Stan had his furniture business, I had my American nail salon, and I buzzed around in a little MR2, which I loved.

Then one morning, I woke up to find Stan pacing about the room. I looked at the clock - it was four thirty. *"What's going on, Stan?"* I asked him sleepily. He said he had cramp, told me not to worry, and said to go back to sleep. I drifted back to sleep, and when I woke up again, he was gone. When I rang him, he said he had something to do, he'd be busy for a while, but would be home that evening.

I got up and pulled my dressing gown on. It was one of those cold, misty mornings that called for hot drinks and fluffy slippers. In the kitchen, I stood waiting for the kettle to boil. Our dog was scratching at the back door, so I let him out and finished making tea, standing at the kitchen counter, stirring the milk around as I thought about Leon. Some days, the thought of him would catch me unawares, and I'd spend some time just thinking about him. It would make me sad, but I was also grateful for our nice life and some peace after all the years of chaos.

On my way into the kitchen, I'd noticed a red car parked across the road with two men in it. I thought they were Old Bill. Walking back through the living room now, I could see the car had gone, but in my mind, the penny dropped, and I realised that's why Stan was always keeping an eye on the window.

When you grow up rough, crime is a common path to choose, but even if you eventually go straight, you're always on your guard. It's like a built-in switch that's installed with your first bit of naughtiness, and it's not something you lose.

I'd taken my tea to bed and was just contemplating life when there was a loud banging on the front door. It sounded like a massive fist, and I thought the police were about to raid us. I could hear the dog going crazy in the garden, and feeling sick, I went down to open the door. The neighbours would be delightfully curtain-twitching, so I'd rather get this over and done with.

When I opened the door, I froze. Standing there were two massive figures in dark overcoats. They looked like hitmen. Barging in, the first one grabbed my arm and put a gun to my head. The one behind him had a massive scar down his face. I saw it as he closed and locked the front door.

*Oh, fuck,* I thought.

The one holding my arm was trying to walk me down the hall, but my legs were jelly. They just wouldn't work. I was like a dead weight, but this man-mountain pulled me easily enough. Then Scarface went all around the house, checking the rooms. I didn't know what they wanted, and it crossed my mind that they were going to rape me. With the size of them, I thought I wouldn't survive it.

Scarface asked me where Stan was.

"Where is Mister Stan?" he said in a Russian accent.

Well, I genuinely didn't know, so I shook my head. He moved his head close to mine, tilted it to the side, and looked me in the eye.

"Call him," he said.

The intensity of it all got to me, and instead of screaming in fear, I shouted at him, "What the fuck do you want?"

"Our money," he said.

*Oh, shit. That can't be good.* That's what I was thinking.

To my relief, Stan answered when I called. I told him there were two men in the house and one of them had a gun to my head. He went quiet for a second before launching into a story. He sounded scared and was talking fast … something about a parcel from Holland that had been stopped. Something about half a million pounds. The half a million-pound statement sank into me like a bullet - if that kind of money was involved, I had no doubt what these men were capable of.

Scarface had taken the phone from me and held it up to his ear, just listening. I couldn't hear what Stan said, but when the phone went down, Scarface looked at Man Mountain and said, *"Two hours."*

While I didn't know the full story, I did know it had something to do with Jean. Every cell in my body was telling me that.

After the pushing and shoving, we'd ended up in the kitchen and I asked to make tea. They said it was fine, and I offered them one, but they refused. We sat in silence, and all I could hear was the tick-tocking of our kitchen clock. It was irritating. The dog had stopped barking a long time ago, but he looked in every now and then, just checking before running off and tearing up the grass.

Thinking they might not kill me if I was nice to them, I offered them tea every twenty minutes or so until they said yes. The 'yes' was like a little victory for me. When I got the milk out of the fridge, my eyes fell on a great big block of cheddar. Everyone likes cheese, don't they? So, without asking, I made a stack of sandwiches because men who looked like that never ate just one.

I put the mugs and plates down in front of them. Man-mountain had put the gun down on the counter, and while I didn't like the sight of it, I preferred seeing it there to having it pressed against my head. Nobody spoke. Scarface was watching the clock. Seconds ticked by - they felt like hours. And then, a hand the size of a shovel reached out and picked up a sandwich. I felt so relieved. Was that a sign it was all going to be alright? Could a cheese sandwich save my life? Should I have put pickle in it for the win?

Praying Stan would get the money and hurry home was how I spent my time, but knowing he turned to drink in times of trouble, I was also praying he didn't get on it and bury this problem under a sea of Patron.

You might ask how I felt. Well, I'm not sure. Should I be angry that he'd left me in the house with two gangsters and their guns? Did he think it would be best not to come back, leaving me to win them over and smooth things out? Or did he know they only wanted the money and holding me hostage was just a scare tactic? He must have been so sure they wouldn't hurt me to not come home, but it was a rotten thing to do.

That day ticked by in long, torturous seconds. I made countless cups of tea. The men took turns going out into the garden for cigarettes, never leaving me alone. Our traitor dog decided he liked them and sat by them while they smoked. When I went to the bathroom, I had to leave my phone on the counter, and one of them would wait outside the door for me. We eventually sat in the living room, and I put the TV on as I couldn't stand the silence. Every twenty minutes or so, Scarface would make a phone call or take one, but he spoke in Russian, and I had no idea what he was saying.

After a few hours, we struck up a conversation. They asked me how long I'd been with Stan, and when I started to tell them, the floodgates opened, and everything came rushing out. I told them how good it had been in the beginning but how it had turned crazy. I told them about him breaking my nose and then how I got my throat cut. And then I told them about Leon and how destroyed I'd been by his death. I said I didn't even care if they shot me because part of me already felt dead inside. Maybe they didn't understand all of what I said but man-mountain shook his head and said something like, *"I can't believe he would leave you like this."*

Late that night, Stan finally called and said he had the money. The Russians got up to leave, and before he closed the door behind him, Scarface turned to me and said, *"Stan does not deserve a good woman like you."* I knew he was right.

Stan and I were coming to the end of our rocky road, and we couldn't go on because around the corner, there was only a cliff.

I sold the beauty salon. Put an offer in on a flat in Chafford Hundred.

Focussed on evolving Playgirlz, our dance troupe. And started nurturing my wild side.

And that's how I ended up in a club with Sophie Ellis Bextor's head spinning like a spaceship.

# 9 PLAYGIRLZ

The new flat was in a development, built in a square around a big fountain. Looking at it, I just knew one day we'd have a foam party in it.

But before then, Paul came to decorate, and Toni was going to rent it from me. I'd told Stan we had to move to London, or we were done. We both knew we were on our last legs, and I never saw much of him anymore because he stayed out all night. My time was spent between Exeter and Essex, finalising things in one and preparing things in the other. Then, on one very ordinary day when Stan had stayed out all night, I packed all my stuff and moved.

From the minute I started living in Essex, I loved it. Playgirlz were going from strength to strength. We had a producer, and we were doing live PAs. I was the MC, Chloe was the singer, Toni the DJ, and Alysha and my cousin were the dancers. We released a remix and music video of 'Money Talks,' and it did well – they even played it on Kiss FM.

For the first time in my life, there was no one to look after apart from myself. No mum to nurse sober, no brothers to keep out of prison, no boyfriend to worry about. The realisation that I could focus purely on me was like a rush, and I threw myself into practising being wild and free.

It was easy to get into London and I'd started hanging out in Mayfair. That's where I met a nice man called Nigel who'd been introduced to me by MC Kai, someone I'd known for years. We had a great night dancing and chatting, and after, the conversation moved to My Space. I knew Nigel was a football player; I just didn't know he was a famous one.

On our first date, he drove to Essex and picked me up in an R8 convertible, but he didn't bring me flowers. Instead, he turned up with a coffee machine from Selfridges and it was so posh, I could never find the pods for it locally. The car should have given me a clue about who he was, but it didn't.

Neither of us knew Chafford Hundred well, but Toni worked in a local pub, so I'd suggested we went there. Little did I know that pub was a West Ham supporters' stronghold and the minute we walked through the door, I felt Nigel hesitate, and then he said, *"Oh no."* The whole pub turned to look at us, and the place went silent. Then someone shouted, "NIGEL QUASHIE, NIGEL QUASHIE!" and the whole pub broke into a chant.

It had been Ted Terry who'd started it, and he was off his nut. We couldn't really leave, so we stayed for one drink, but it was uncomfortable. Ted Terry was getting handsy, trying to grab hold of me, and everyone kept coming over to talk to Nigel. It wasn't the best first date, but it didn't spoil the connection we had, and we carried on seeing each other. I later found out that pub was also a dealer pub - you'd think I'd be more clued up about these things, wouldn't you? It wasn't long before Ted Terry got done for cocaine dealing after trying to sell it to undercover reporters there. That was plastered all over the papers, and I felt bad for him. I knew what that was like.

Dating Nigel was easy. He was a sweet, kind man and not at all full of himself - even with all his talent, he was humble. Since West Ham's training ground wasn't far from me, he'd often turn up at mine in his kit.

I was still in my wild and free phase, and at weekends, I partied hard. Toni told me once that Nigel had called me a wreck head. Apparently, he'd said he would have married me if I wasn't. I wouldn't have married anyone then, no matter who it was, as I was far too intoxicated by freedom, and I wasn't going to let anyone tie me down.

Party life continued, and one night, I was with Toni in Planet Hollywood when we met Turkish actor Tamer Hassan. I didn't know he was an actor; I just thought he was a big, friendly, and very funny guy. His energy was contagious, and he had me laughing constantly. Some people come into your life, and you just know they're there to stay - Tamer was one of them, a cracking good laugh, and an absolute diamond friend.

Toni and I had left our drinks on the bar while we went to dance. After, we went to sit with Tamer and his mates. I was sitting between Jason

Statham and my sister Toni, and Sophie Ellis-Bextor was across the table on the sofa next to Tamer. We were chatting away, and Jason had just asked me where we were going after when I looked across at Sophie and her head had turned into a spaceship.

I felt dizzy and a little bit sick and I started blinking, trying to refocus my eyes, desperate to make Sophies head look like its beautiful self. It wasn't working. My mouth was heavy, like it was stuffed with cotton wool, and I felt like the me inside was shrinking into the other me inside. It was so weird. Gripping Toni's hand, I squeezed it tight.

She could see something was very wrong, and so she carefully pulled me up to make it look like we were just going to the bathroom, then guided me outside into the fresh air. I didn't sober up. My drink had been spiked, and I don't really remember anything else about that night. Toni got me home, and I was so grateful for that, but I'd been really looking forward to partying all night. Oh, and Jason if you're reading this, I'm sorry - it was nothing personal.

At that time, I was on the tail end of dating Nigel, but it ended soon after when the press ran a kiss-and-tell story from his 'other' girlfriend. There was a little karma in that, and that's okay. It's how it should be. But I won't deny that I had feelings for Nigel, and it hurt a bit. He was a nice man, and he'd treated me like a queen. Our time together was perfect for me, especially after the hurricane of a relationship I'd had with Stan. Nigel had been just what I needed, and I'm grateful he came into my life when he did.

But here I was again. Single, but happy about it, and 'wild' me was riding the party vibe hard.

Essex had been so good for me, and I was also glad I got to share it all with my sister. We'd host great parties at the flat, and while they were all crazy good, there was one that will go down in history. The Artful Dodger, DJ Luck, and MC DT were all there, and it was going off.

Sunday morning rolled around, all the doors and windows were open, people were dancing on the balcony, the neighbours had their doors open and were dancing on theirs, and someone had put washing-up liquid in the fountain. Everyone rushed down and started dancing in it. Bubbles and great big clumps of white foam floated around; it was just the best time. It was the kind of party people talk about for the rest of their lives – legendary.

As I owned the house, there was no landlord to tell me what I could and couldn't do, and we lived in a young professional community - no families with children, which was lucky.

Music was life, and I loved making it in the studio with the girls. We were smashing it, and I never wanted the partying to end, so I took my wild side to Notting Hill Carnival.

And that's how I ended up creating life with a legend who went down in British history.

# 10 SKIBADEE

Around twenty years ago, our dance troupe, Playgirlz, were in the studio making music. It was late August, the sun was shining, and we were flying high. We'd had a great studio session, and as we were in West London, we decided to finish up and go to Notting Hill Carnival. I was so excited as I'd never been before, and from the moment we got on the train, it was one long party. The streets were alive with music, soaking into every pore and every pavement. We walked - no, we danced from Westbourne Grove Station, through Portobello Road, heading towards the canal at Kensal Rise. But before we got there, we heard the familiar beat of drum & bass, so we followed it, and it led all the way to my destiny.

The man had the crowd in the palm of his hand - spitting bars that hit people like a bolt of electricity. They were going wild. He was mesmerising, and I couldn't take my eyes off him. This may sound weird, but he also looked kind, do you know what I mean? Maybe I was getting high from the weed-filled air around us?

We never made it to the canal that day. We hung around until he finished his set, and I ended up chatting to MC Skibadee about music and Playgirlz. Swapping Facebook details was how we left it, and we started chatting on Messenger every now and then. He would always ask me how the family was, and I liked that. I thought it was a sign that he was kind and caring, but I wasn't daft - I knew he had a bit of a reputation as a ladies' man, and I needed to be cautious.

Like all friendships, the years rolled by quickly. Sometimes we'd chat a lot, and sometimes not much at all - it was the typical Facebook friendship.

A few years later, I went to the 'We Are Festival' with my girls, and Skibadee was headlining. I knew he'd been making a name for himself and had been playing to thousands of fans across Europe. I was also looking forward to seeing Harry Shotta and Macky Gee. We were backstage partying with Bugzy Malone and his security team when I saw Skiba. He seemed pleased to see me, and we grabbed a quick chat before he headed off to his next rave. Before he left, he asked me to go along later but we were having a party at mine that night,

We got back to mine and set everything up and Bugzy pulled up in his Rolls-Royce Phantom about twenty minutes later. The party started off great, then he got into it with a ginger nut neighbour of mine, and I didn't want the drama. Skiba had been messaging me from his gig at Breaking Science, so I decided to go.

We Playgirlz left the party and grabbed a cab to South London and as soon as we got there, Carly, the owner, took me straight over to Skiba. He had a proper grin on his face as he pulled me in close for a kiss, and I think I blushed. In the smoking area, he pulled me onto his lap, and we sat cuddling. So many girls came over to chat to him, but no matter what they looked like or what they said, not once did he stop cuddling me. It made me feel worth something.

Watching the man on stage was like watching a magic show, and it kind of swept me off my feet. When the gig finished, we went back to mine, and later, at the party comedown, when everyone was hanging and chatting, he made an announcement. In front of everyone, he said, "I'm going to change Cheree's life. She needs a baby, and I'm gonna give her one."

The funny thing was nobody disputed it. Crazy as it sounded, this made me happy, and after that party, we were inseparable. We were also well on the way to fulfilling his prophecy by having the most amazing sex - at it like rabbits we were.

Our lifestyle developed around the parties, gigs, and raves, and just like every other couple, we had our ups and downs. We were learning where to draw the lines, where to push the boundaries, where to give and take. When we were apart, he liked to know where I was always, and he'd message me constantly. But then, we were in that early stage where butterflies and greener pastures lead you down a rose-coloured view of love.

On full throttle, we decided to move in together and viewed a stunning sea-view apartment in Rochester that had a concierge and a gym. St Mary's Bay was a beautiful place, and one of my good friends lived close by. Laura had been in my life since we first met at the clinic where I had a bum lift, and she'd been there for me through all the highs and lows. She also got on well with Skiba, which was a bonus - you know what it's like when your mates don't get on with your man. I hate that. We were as tight as any friends who have partied hard in Ibiza and knew the kind of secrets about each other that make you friends for life - what happens in Ibiza stays in Ibiza.

Life was on track. That's how I felt about it. My beauty business was booming, and I'd been working with a lot of celebrity clients, many from reality TV shows. Callum Izzard from *Ibiza Weekender* had become a good friend, but Skiba was a little paranoid about our friendship. Yes, Callum is very handsome, but he is also a lovely lad, and I wanted Skiba to get on with him. I hoped he would see that we were just good friends.

The opportunity for them to meet came about when Skiba's daughter, Aysha, was coming to stay for the weekend. She was mad for Callum, so I got Skiba to bring her to the salon for a facial when Callum was there. When they turned up, Callum's handsome face was covered in a big white facemask. I soon cleaned him up and watched Aysha loving on him - it was very cute. After that I took her for a bit of spoiling at Amy G's Salon in Ockendon. They had a lot of celebrity clients and Aysha was beaming at having her nails done there. She always asked questions about the beauty business, and I think it interested her as a career, so I was always happy to encourage her.

That first meeting between the boys had also gone well, which was great news because I'd been brewing an idea in my head. As we were party people, we understood the one thing other party people didn't like - hangovers. I wanted something to prevent them and had come up with a pill idea that Skiba named *Freshheadz*. The three of us chatted it over, and I knew Callum would be the perfect person to bring in on the product. Pretty soon, *Freshheadz* were in play.

Now we needed to put together a launch party, so we combined resources and came up with a great celebrity guest list to help promote the brand. At that time, Macky Gee was seeing my PA Bex, and he jumped on as the party DJ. Both Pioneer and Sam Supplier did sets. The champagne flowed, the *TOWIE* girls were in, the press were in, and even Skiba's family were in. The night went off like a rocket. Everyone said it was the best party they'd ever been to, and of course, we made sure they all took their *Freshheadz* before bed.

Laura and D were giving us a lift home, but he was off his nut. He started kicking off as he was driving, then there was a huge bang, causing us to skid and swerve. We realised the wheel had come off.

Luckily, we hadn't been going fast, or it could have been far worse. Skiba and I got out and started walking down the motorway. We were just happy, high, and holding hands as the sun came up, and that's a memory I keep in my heart for rainy days.

Freshheadz had been a massive success. The press did a fantastic job with the story, and the reviews were brilliant. Sales exploded.

Don't you find that when life is going great, there's always something not so great to niggle you? For me, at that time, it was hearing that Skiba had another child with his first love. It was Skiba's friend Axe who let that slip, and when I asked Skiba about it, he denied it intensely, so I left it alone.

That was the only niggle. Everything else was blissful, even the ordinary day-to-day. One night, I'd got home from work, and Laura was chatting to Skiba in the kitchen. He was cooking a steak dinner, and I remember thinking how a regular day like that was one of the foundations of the life you build. I felt like we'd got it right. When Laura left that night, she kissed me on the cheek and whispered, "I've never seen you so happy."

And I was. Probably the happiest I'd ever been. That made me wonder if you could be so happy that you jinx yourself?

Not long after that, I was cleaning and dusting Skiba's laptop, which was open. When I ran a feather duster over the keyboard, the screen lit up, and the first thing I saw was a photo of a girl playing with herself. Then there was a stream of messages between him and other girls, and as I flicked through them, my lovely little world came undone. He had become my everything, and we had a hugely intimate relationship where we could talk about anything. And it couldn't have been for the lack of sex because our sex life was incredible... so what had happened? Deep in my heart, I was reminded of days when Dad came for my brothers, leaving me watching from the window as they drove away. This hurt like that, and I was devastated.

When I questioned him, he justified it. He said he'd been single for a long time, so naturally, there'd be hundreds of messages and photos on his laptop. A lot of these girls were his fans, and I knew how much he loved his fans, but there was a line. The girls in the photos looked dirty, and they were doing dirty things – to me, it seemed like he had a secret online life. We argued fiercely about it, but he kept saying it wasn't what I thought.

Christmas came, and we stayed home together. It was just the two of us for a whole week, and we indulged in all the good things, including each other. There was much food, much drink, and so much sex that we had the best time. We also spent a lot of time watching videos and chatting till the early hours, putting the world to rights. That is when he opened up to me about his online life. He explained that he'd been doing it for as long as he'd done music. His career was everything to him, and he wanted to give it everything, which meant a real relationship would get in the way. But things were different now. He was in a real relationship, but his old habits were hanging around, and most of them had slutty dress sense.

After Christmas, he went to New Zealand for a gig, I went to Australia to see my brother, and we planned to meet up in Thailand.

I'd been at my brothers for a few days, and we'd been staying up till the early hours, drinking and catching up. But one morning, I woke up feeling sick, and it didn't feel like a hangover. The sickness carried on all day, and it was my sister-in-law who said, "You're not pregnant, are you?"

Alarm bells went off in my head, and I couldn't remember when my last period had been. My sister-in-law bundled me in the car, and we went out to get a test. It was positive. I sent my brother out to buy more tests as I didn't believe it, but they were all positive too.

Skiba had always said he was going to give me a baby, and he was so very sure of it, but when it finally sank in for me, I knew it was a God-given blessing. I wanted to share the news with him immediately, but I couldn't get through to him.

Sticking to our original plan, I took two planes and lugged two big suitcases around while panicking about losing the baby. The journey was difficult, but I made it to Bangkok feeling anxious. I still couldn't get hold of him, and I was so tired that I just broke down in tears and asked a passer-by if they could help me. Bless that man. He got me to the departure lounge, and when I got through to the plane, there they were – Shabba and Skiba. The minute he saw me, he came rushing over, grabbed me tight, and pulled me close. That calmed me down.

The relief was massive. I was looking forward to seeing Shabba's girl Zoe again – I'd met her at a massive SASAS gig in Manchester a while before and we'd got on well. But funny story about Zoe, at that gig she'd given me some of her water and it was laced with MDNA – I got so off my nut that I jumped on stage and told Skiba to get off because I thought was taking over my gig with the UHF dancers - he had the right hump with me for a day or two.  That was the first time I met Jemma Lucy too and all three of us had a lot of fun. Zoe was quite posh and sounded like she came from money, but she'd been to public school, so that explained it. Zoe also had a passion for drum and bass, and she'd gone from Shabba's fan to Shabba's girl and now we were just two gals in paradise with a couple of music legends.

Waking up to a blue-green sea every day was soothing for the soul, and my body felt grateful. But it was feeling a lot of things I wasn't used to, down to the little babe hitching a ride in my belly. We'd planned this holiday for our party personalities, but mine had been left behind in Australia. Skiba's was still very much with him.

So, while I should have been having the best time, I couldn't.

Skiba wanted to stay up all night smoking weed with the guys, but I didn't want to be anywhere near it. He was always energised and hyped up, and I was always tired and wanting to sleep. None of the plans we'd made were now suited to me.

We were supposed to be raving, but I just wasn't feeling it. I'd lost a baby before, and I was terrified it would happen again. Every night there was a party going on somewhere, and I could hear it from our room. The music, splashes from the pool, whistles, just general hard-partying noise – I knew everyone was having an amazing time, but all I wanted to do was lay around.

There were some nice times, like the day we spent riding around the island on a scooter. I'd been a bit nervous about being on the bike, but Skiba turned out to be a safe driver, and we had a lovely time riding around the coast through stunning landscapes. We'd stopped for lunch, taking in the views, and soaking up the sun as we ate, but then we saw the police. And they were headed straight for us. My stomach flipped – what now?

Funny story – they thought Skiba was a 'Lookie Lookie' man harassing a blonde tourist. He'd gone so dark in the sun that they were convinced of it, but when we showed them his Instagram account, they were all smiles and asked to have a photo with us.

Another great day was the body-painting day that was organised by Jay, the Tour Manager. And I did make it to a couple of the gigs – they were amazing, while I could keep my eyes open, but whenever I was around all that loud noise, I'd pray to Leon, asking him to keep my baby safe.

When it was time to leave the island, we went by boat, and it was terrifying. The waves got so big; they were like giants attacking the sky. I spent the whole journey gripping the sides of my seat.

Then we were back in the UK, and I thought my body would settle down. It didn't. I felt so sick, and I was having trouble breathing, so Skiba got me an ambulance, and they scanned me at the hospital. Everything was fine with the baby, and that was all that really mattered. I had some cold, flu, chesty cough combination, and the doctors thought I might be at risk of pneumonia, so they told me to stay in bed and rest. We got back to the UK just as the country was going into the pandemic, so, I think I had covid.

Then lockdown hit us hard. All of us. Personally, I was relieved that the world stopped, and I didn't have to work or stress. There was no need to rush back and forth across the Dartford Bridge every day, and all I had to do was stay home, look after myself, and enjoy my pregnancy. I was looking forward to that.

At the flat, we'd set up a studio for Skiba, and he worked happily on his music. I'd rest, and together, we'd go for slow walks around the lake and do whatever shopping we were allowed to do. When the world got quiet and people were locked down together, it was a true test of compatibility, and we really were. Music kept him upbeat, and he wanted to share that, so he started an online show called 'Breakfast with Skibadee' on a Saturday morning. It had started with him playing Drum & Bass and chatting about various DJs, then it evolved naturally into deep chats about life and lockdown. Soon, thousands of people were listening in, many of whom had been struggling with being imprisoned at home or feeling the emptiness of being alone. Skiba was a wordsmith, and he knew just what to say – he really helped people through, and it was as good for him as it was for them.

We'd got ourselves into a routine by then. I was happily pregnant and getting bigger by the minute, and Skiba was enjoying home life, especially as I mothered him a bit, making him breakfast and smoothies. We were taking care of each other and looking forward to the day we would become three. Because of my age, I had to have some special tests, and when the lady called us with the results, she let it slip that we were having a girl. I burst into tears, and she asked me if they were tears of happiness, but I couldn't lie. "I wanted a boy," I told her.

Worrying is what pregnant women do, but I felt better after booking a private scan and when we saw our baby on the screen together, it was magical. We were both brought to tears, and Skiba turned to me, promising I would see a massive change in him and there'd be no more chatting to girls. "Cheree," he said, "we're going to make it."

He meant it then. I have no doubt about that. If only lockdown had lasted longer, then the change that was taking place inside him could have got a deeper grip. If only it could have sunk right down into his bones and set like cement. If it had, we would have made it...

But Skiba had developed a thirst that could never be satisfied, and its name was Peckham. I don't know what he did there, but it seemed to have power over him. When he was craving it, the atmosphere around him changed, getting heavier and darker. There'd be shadows in his eyes, and he'd get irritated about little things, then he'd turn nasty. This sometimes happened during a live show, and my phone would be full of messages asking, "What's wrong with him? Is he off his head? Is he taking drugs? What is Skiba on tonight?" I was worried.

After a show like that, I'd asked him outright if he'd taken anything. He confessed to having a little line and said he'd just needed some energy. That made me angry, and I told him he didn't need to do that on a Saturday night when he was home with his pregnant girlfriend. Then it started happening in the week too, and soon, he was running to Peckham and not coming home for a day or two. Nor would he answer my messages. That's not what you need from your baby daddy when you're pregnant.

One of those nights, I started to feel rough. My head was killing me, and I felt like I had a temperature. You know how it is when you're pregnant, you can't even take paracetamol, and of course, I was worried – it's natural. I texted and rang several times, but he didn't answer or reply, and that is when the rot set in. When he was home, he was distant, and he could turn nasty in a split second. I saw an aggressive side to him, and it surprised me – this was not the man I'd met at Notting Hill Carnival. It wasn't Skiba. Something else had got inside him – a devil in the form of addiction held him in a grip, and he'd find any excuse to cause an argument, just so he could fuck off to Peckham.

And when he was at home, I'd catch him on his phone and see messages over his shoulder, and I knew he'd been talking to women all night while I slept next to him, keeping his baby safe. The harsh reality was, I couldn't trust him.

Heartbroken. Devastated. Wounded. Those were all the things I felt when I asked him, "What the fuck is going on?" But instead of talking to me, he went mad, grabbed the keys off the table as if he was going out, but then, in rage, threw them at my head. It started bleeding. I stood there with my mouth open, as I couldn't believe he'd done it.

When he'd come down from the gear, he said sorry, but it was too late. Even when he got down on his hands and knees begging me for another chance, I couldn't say yes. I had no way of knowing if any of those online girls had turned into in-the-flesh girls in Peckham. We hadn't had sex for ages, so I thought it was quite possible.

When he realised I'd had enough, he started trying hard. Isn't it always the way? Constantly apologising, going out of his way to be kind and look after me. He'd make me breakfast every morning, go to the shops with me, and he went back to being happy and content in his studio at home. What I have found the saddest about all of this is that we had everything we could need for a great life together – we could have smashed it. I told him that, and he agreed, so we decided a fresh start might help, and it was his job to find us a bigger place to live.

The size was most important, as I wanted to close my Lakeside clinic and set one up at home. For that we needed at least four bedrooms. One to sleep in, one for our baby, one for his studio, and one for my clinic. Finding it was his mission and I hoped it would keep him away from Peckham.

If I'd had any idea – even the slightest hint of what my life might look like a year later, I would have done anything to prevent it – I'd have sold my soul to the devil if necessary, and why not? I'd already been to hell

and back, and I'd rather face that a hundred times than go through what

happened then...

# ABOUT THE AUTHOR

Cheree Leon is a reality TV personality, Influencer, and businesswoman. As the partner of legendary MC Skibadee who has sadly passed, and mum to his daughter Skylar, Cheree focuses on being a good mum while juggling a fast-paced career. She's responsible for keeping many celebrity faces looking so good and, to give back, she founded the Aesthetic Circle, where the truly deserving, can stop for a minute, get pampered and think about themselves for once.

This is her first book, but the story doesn't end here. Part two is already underway, as is the film script...

9 781739 893088